...God's Turn

S. Wronski

WESTBOW·
P R E S S
A DIVISION OF THOMAS NELSON
& ZONDERVAN

WestBow Press books may be ordered through booksellers or by contacting:

WestBow Press
A Division of Thomas Nelson & Zondervan
1663 Liberty Drive
Bloomington, IN 47403
www.westbowpress.com
1 (866) 928-1240

Because of the dynamic nature of the Internet, any web addresses or
links contained in this book may have changed since publication and
may no longer be valid. The views expressed in this work are solely those
of the author and do not necessarily reflect the views of the publisher,
and the publisher hereby disclaims any responsibility for them.

Any people depicted in stock imagery provided by Thinkstock are models,
and such images are being used for illustrative purposes only.
Certain stock imagery © Thinkstock.

ISBN: 978-1-4908-2537-3 (sc)
ISBN: 978-1-4908-2538-0 (e)

Library of Congress Control Number: 2014902037

Printed in the United States of America.

WestBow Press rev. date: 9/15/2014

A time is soon upon us when all we have seen will let up, and what we believed will have to redeem us. When? Only the Father knows. The signs? Need not be a daunting topic. Are we ready? We ought to prepare. Let us yet again remember the Kingdom of God and defend it unswervingly. Through Christ, we have been taught how to relate with God and with man; through Christ, we can declare:

WE CHOOSE TO GO BACK
TO GOD'S PRESENCE.

Contents

CHAPTER 1: THE RISE OF AN EMPIRE: AN INTRODUCTION

When I was in college, introductory courses thoroughly excited me and I felt comfortable with their relative ease. I could not resist the intrigue of a minuscule discussion on empires, much like an introductory course...

~

Once long ago, Scandinavian Vikings ruled the Russians. Then Asians ruled the Russians. Battles were fought and empires rose and fell; the Byzantine Empire, the Ottoman Turks, the Roman; the British. The history of statehood was written on a tabloid of bloodshed until treaties were formed, alliances forged and trade became the way to co-exist. The world we live in today is by and large a neo-liberal world, which gives it that the minute countries stop trading, the global economy slumps. The forces of globalization have prevailed strong against nations themselves with information, trade and culture knowing no boundaries. Even closed economies and isolated states like North Korea, Cuba- as well as geographically distant states excluded from global trade circles have had some form of contact with the products of globalization. Empire as an earthly pretext thus sounds farcical.

Yet at such a time is the Empire of the Almighty ripe for enlargement, we know it formally as the Kingdom of Heaven, or the Kingdom of God - the Kingdom where Christ is the heir. Like he, it will swallow up death in victory. His empire will last forever and this is granted. In such a time as this, the body of Christ has an opportunity to globalize; reach every circle and vehemently create new ways of livelihood penetrating every society and every age. The time is so ripe for the body of Christ to work round the clock to publish with a voice of thanksgiving, to sing in the congregations and among the unbelieving. Now is such a time to continuously produce new "information technology" that will attract souls to the living and loving God, through His son, Jesus Christ. We will endeavour to do this and be victorious at it. We could start by understanding exactly who we are in Christ- Royalty, then figure out who we are to each other-Kingdom, then master skills, wisdom, courage, boldness and His righteousness, to be able to shout it out loud:

Christ is King and one day every knee will bow and every tongue confess it!

~

For a long time terms such as "Kingdom principles," and the "Kingdom of God" remained common place in my circles and yet ambiguous. What did it mean to be kingdom minded? What did Jesus mean at all when he said, "the Kingdom of God is upon you." What did it mean in the Lord's Prayer to say, "thy Kingdom come?" Then one day a song came back to the back of my head quite randomly, "Righteousness, Peace, Joy in the Holy Ghost... righteousness peace and joy in the Holy Ghost that's the kingdom of God!" It is a scripture; Romans 14:17. We used to harmonize this song in high school and we added a few *pum-pa-riri rarams* in there! I then realized, well that's it! All that Kingdom business was about the righteousness of God himself and God in us, it was about having peace and having a peculiar joy because of the Holy Spirit in us. Joy in the Holy Ghost- that was what probably kept those poor persecuted Christians going strong. The Kingdom of God was upon me! Today still we need to make peace with the Holy Ghost and have joy in him as He is Christ's immediate presence with us. Former Kingdoms were about colonizing, imposing culture and robbing dignity at all costs. They came, they reigned and they failed to last. The Kingdom of God is freely given, and it is a choice. All who are willing and gladly choose it, find the greatest treasures in it. However, how can anyone believe a message he has not received? The Christian therefore has been mandated as the steward of God's kingdom, to speak of this Kingdom, just as John the Baptist spoke of the Christ to come.

Christians cannot force salvation for it is given by God alone; but they have a duty to play: to spread his word and spread his likeness: for indeed empires enlarge.

3

The Kingdom of God is upon us, even this generation, where hearts are hardened and a master called mammon demands so much of our time; a generation spiritually suppressed by pop-culture and the rhetoric of political correctness and inclusion- a generation that is nevertheless ours; and loved by our Maker. Let us build.

*

'For the Kingdom of God is not in word but in power.'
I Corinthians 4:20

The era we are now in is hugely financially circuited and the global economic system is volatile. It is getting more difficult for everyone to achieve the so called dream life; go to school, get a good job, get married, buy a car, buy a house, take your kids on vacations and ensure they also go to college. Attending college is either elusive or entails accruing enormous debt to pay for tuition and textbooks. Jobs are more scarce or concentrated in what we could call elitist professions. Technology is rapidly expanding, if you fail to or do not want to catch-on, you are 'left behind.' Almost everything has become privatized and in every corner someone has started something. Actually if you haven't thought out a business idea by now you're very behind! Churches have not been excluded- buildings that facilitate fellowship need to be paid for, ministers are also living in a world where buying a house and paying bills and living expenses are sky rocketing so they have

4

to also become somewhat competitive just to survive. The line has waxed so thin between fighting for survival as a ministry and being regarded as 'prosperity pimps.' It's truly sad. But it's a wearisome reality. People are suffering and are weary of the financial strains and the demands of this world. The body of Christ needs to fervently heal this weariness in people, bring joy where life is just hard, bring comfort where uncertainty looms and offer a resting place where people can realize that Christ has overcome this world too. Will he not also sustain us supernaturally while we yet have to live in it, then one day, get us out of here?

As Christians, we ought to realize that sometimes people just want help with everyday living. Help someone know how to manage the little money they have, help someone find out about places that can help, or help someone feel good about where they are in life. We have heard a lot about increase, prosperity and favour. Needful now, is power. We need to offer the power of God; the peace of God in Christ and the guidance and joy of the Holy Spirit.

When you become a Christian, it encompasses your whole life. Therefore everything you do, think, say and long for should have a Godly motive and has to be realized as a precious gift from God. Indeed life is God's gift to us, life with meaning and hope for eternity, is Christ's sacrifice for us. We exercise to appreciate life and live it happily under the light of God, not happily according to our fleshly desires. I like how Reverend Steve Elzinga describes our connections to God:

Connection 1- Personal life
The most reliable and consistent method of hearing from God is to read the Bible, His word to us. Your personal connection with God, having a thriving, healthy relationship with Him, is the first step to impacting all the connections with the people in your life.

Connection 2- Marriage
The heart of a marriage connection is a devotional life that fully involves both spouses. When God is a central player in your marriage, your marriage will benefit greatly from God's presence and guidance.

Connection 3- Family
Seeking God together with family helps families to grow closer to each other and to God, to build a firm foundation. When your family takes time to listen to God and talk to God together through family devotions your family grows spiritually.

Connection 4- Fellowship
A vital Christian needs the support of a fellowship connection- your Bible study group, youth group, teams and clubs where together you connect with God. We need that opportunity to be accountable with like-minded Christian friends.

Connection 5- Church

A talking and listening dialogue with God is at the heart of corporate worship and we connect to God in a broad way that involves a wider body of His believers.

Connection 6- Kingdom

Kingdom connectedness is admitting that God rules more than your small slice of the world; it means being involved outside of your local church. It might be as simple as two friends sitting down with a cup of coffee, sharing what is going on in their lives at home, at work and at play. It might be getting involved with a group of likeminded Christians to discuss methods of protecting and preserving the riches of God's creation. It is saying: Let's talk and listen- connect to God together and see where He is leading us.

Connection 7- World

Be prepared to share with those who do not yet have a connection to God. Inviting people to participate in talking and listening to God alongside you is a daily, stable, relational, Scriptural, and reproducible entry into the Christian faith. It doesn't take any special talent or training, just a willingness to do what you do in your everyday life with someone else.

And so the kingdom of God is very impartial and open to all. There are amusing parables in the gospels as to how Christ likened the kingdom of heaven. In Matthew 18, the kingdom is portrayed in terms of a forgiveness haven. In chapter 20, it is likened to a householder who hired labourers at different times during the day, gave them all the same terms of employment, and paid all the first ones to start work and the last ones to start work, the same wage. Christ ends this parable by saying, *"So the last shall be first, and the first last: for many be called, but few chosen." (Matt 20:16)* I see the undertones of the Jew-Gentile story in that verse. In Matthew 25, the kingdom of heaven is likened to the famous ten virgins; the five foolish did not prepare but went to meet the bridegroom with no oil (the Holy Spirit) in their lamps and slept while waiting; when the bells began to ring they did not have oil in their lamps to show them their way to the marriage ceremony and were left and the doors shut. In the same chapter, he goes on to tell the parable of the servants who were given a different number of talents according to ability. Some invested in their talents and they produced fruit for the master, one servant hid his talent and it yielded nothing. In verses 29-34, Jesus informs us;

"For unto every one that hath shall be given, and he shall have abundance: but from him that hath not shall be taken away even that which he hath. And cast ye the unprofitable servant into outer darkness: there shall be weeping and gnashing of teeth. When the Son of man shall come in his glory, and all the holy angels with him, then shall he sit upon the throne of his glory: And before him shall be gathered all nations: and he shall separate them one from another, as a shepherd divideth his sheep from

the goats: And he shall set the sheep on his right hand, but the goats on the left. Then shall the King say unto them on his right hand, Come ye blessed of my Father, inherit the kingdom prepared for you from the foundation of the world."

I love the way Jesus builds up this visual of the kingdom; he first shows how it is about forgiveness of all sin (debt) and shows how anyone can come into it, not just the first and experienced ones in the things of God- anyone. It is however a vineyard or a household to be worked in. Then he shows how clearly there is a mandate to keep your light burning and to watch and wait for the day of the second coming of the Lord. When that day comes our actions shall be weighed based on the abilities endowed on us and our ability to recognize what has been given to us. What a story-line. In essence: do not be a goat.

As described above, the kingdom of God is about conduct to one another and reverence to a master, who is a loving and just God. A time will come when Jesus' coronation occurs, and that is the day he will establish everything holy, everything peaceful, righteous and glorious. Much like climate change, people have been talking about it for years, many remain nonchalant, but it is so clear that winters are no longer the same and summers keep breaking records. It makes sense to prepare for the kingdom by working towards the goals of righteousness, peace and joy with the Holy Ghost as our guide; and not people's beliefs or non-beliefs! The guidelines are laid before us in the bible. Reflecting on the God-head mystery, we hear the Great I Am saying, my turn...

I have often been a glaring participant in horror stories about immigrants who cannot speak English, steal jobs, smell funny and are ever critical about their supposedly new home countries. I once excitedly asked a friend to take me on the subway in London, and at every stop I found myself thinking yes Britain should really close its borders, ruing at the boomerang effect of the Imperial rule.

There is no better feeling than a sense of belonging, and entitlement. Knowing that your mere life is deemed important and knowing that even if you make a thousand wrong turns, there is a place where everyone in it enjoys you…

~

There was a man of Pharisee, his name was called Nicodemus. He came to Jesus one night and said, 'How can a man be born again?' Does that story ring a bell? In John 3:5 Jesus further tells Nicodemus, *'Verily, verily, I say unto thee, Except a man be born of water and of the Spirit, he cannot enter into the kingdom of God.'*

We need to carefully study everything surrounding those words. We now know that the kingdom of God is righteousness, peace and joy in the Holy Ghost and a time is coming when it will be completely established, Christ being the heir when this world ends. The scripture above reveals the two pre-requisites for becoming a citizen of this kingdom:

Being born of water refers to water baptism, and being born of the Spirit, Holy Spirit baptism. If you are spiritual, you probably know just how frustrating it is to explain spiritual things to someone who does not subscribe to the same beliefs. When you mature in your relationship with God, there are certain things you just cannot do, and certain things you *must* do, like forgiving, praying at all times, praying in the spirit, speaking life and carefully watching what words come out of your mouth as the devil can use those words to curse you. Ever known someone very rebellious, spiteful of biblical principles and oblivious to how what we speak out can have spiritual ramifications? For the most part, you will find that such people have not yet been baptized and made that solid decision to lay their own lives down, for Jesus to live and reign in them. See there is something about dying to self that opens the door to understanding Godliness.

Except a man be born of water and of the Spirit, he cannot enter into the kingdom of God.

Imagine even starting that one, 'You need to be baptized to get it!' If God spoke, and light was created, and we are made in His image, why is it difficult to understand that our words have power?

Before Christ started his ministry, the first thing he did was to be baptized to fulfill the scriptures as He put it. Just after he got baptized, the Spirit came descending like a dove on him. He first got water baptized, then the Holy Spirit came down upon him. Baptism is the rite of passage for every Christian. I just came to understand this concept and it is blowing my mind away, and all I want to do is get all my family baptized, all my friends and hopefully enemies too. My pastor Surekha Natta put it this way, "When a man tells you he wants to marry you, he does not come to you and say, 'You are now my wife,' rather he presents a ring and a marriage certificate is issued, he has to do something that can prove that he is now your husband." It is the same thing with Christianity. It is not enough to say the prayer of salvation and go out and say, I am a Christian. Baptism, is your public, emotional and spiritual way of dying to self and saying, I have laid my own life down and now Christ is alive in me. Baptism is very crucial to the kingdom of God. The word of God says in John 3:23 that no man can enter the kingdom without baptism by water and baptism by spirit – you have to die to self first before God's spirit can live and flourish in you. The verses below explain it.

"[…] we also joy in God through our Lord Jesus Christ, by whom we have now received the atonement. Wherefore, as by one man (Adam) sin entered into the world, and death by sin; and so death passed upon all men...(19) For as by one man's disobedience many were made sinners, so

*by the obedience of one shall many be made righteous..."
(Romans 5:11-12)*

"Knowing this that our old man is crucified with him, that the body of sin might be destroyed, that henceforth we should not serve sin. For he that is dead is freed from sin. Now if we be dead with Christ, we believe that we shall also live with him." (Romans 6:6)

We are 'dead with Christ' by being *"...buried with him by baptism into death: that like as Christ was raised up from the dead by the glory of the Father, even so we also should walk in newness of life." (Romans 6:4)*

"Likewise reckon ye also yourselves to be dead indeed unto sin, but alive unto God through Jesus Christ our Lord. Let not sin therefore reign in your mortal body, that ye should obey it in the lusts thereof." (Romans 6:11)

"Being then made free from sin, ye become the servants of righteousness." (Romans 6:18)

When we get baptised and die to our flesh, our erstwhile passions lose ground to the passion of the Christ: to do the father's will. We become the servants of righteousness meaning whatever thing is right before God, we do.

Show me your papers?

So after we have openly confessed Christ and gone

down in the water as a sign of sacrificing our fleshly lusts to take up a life in Christ, Christ is free to operate in us. Yes in the days of the law God instructed atonement and sacrificial rituals, altar building and offering giving. Thankfully Christ's blood atoned for all sin and we can all now freely go before God for anything, but remember that even in the new testament He is still the same God, He still does have a bunch of odd things He requires us to do out of obedience and love for Him. So after being water baptized one more step is needed, to be really waiting to hear from God and to *want* to hear from God. This is the baptism of the Holy Spirit. Sadly, many Christians miss this step and in Jesse Duplantis' words, settle for the 'garment of salvation and never obtain the robe of righteousness.' I cannot find another way to put it, preachers, church leaders, Sunday School teachers and parents need to hold Holy Spirit sessions. This is where you fast for God's spirit to come down on children, on cities and on nations. This is where you let go of all your thoughts, worries and preoccupations and just look to hear from God. This is when you say, here I am God, speak to me, direct me and work through me. This is where it starts to get uncomfortable for those who only thought signing up for Christianity was a green card. Not so, my dear. If you want to be a Christian, it means you are now at war with Satan. You are taking up arms to defend the kingdom of God and a restoration of man's authority over what God has granted him. It means you are ready to want to know and see the fiery darts of the wicked one, the snares and tricks of the devil. Peter warns how we fight not against flesh and blood, but against principalities and powers of darkness. The devil fell out, he knows that time is running out, so he is on a quest to make as many of God's children fall out too. On our own we do not have the power to overcome him, that is why Christ came and did not fail God as the first Adam, just so his shed blood would atone for mankind's sin, and win a fair game for God to forgive the human race. In Christ we see that a life of doing only God's will; is possible. In Christ, we saw that when thanks was given to God, acknowledging Him as the All in All, provision would multiply, the sick got healed, evil spirits were cast out, and many that were broken and outcast, found true love, and true happiness.

When we ask Jesus into our lives, we are simply making a choice, to follow after his example, so that we can return to God, His Father, to whom He kept all focus. The most fascinating thing is Christ was God himself, in human form! He loves us that much, and decided to come down to us in person, to show us how to come back to Him! What's even better; in His kingdom, God does not intend to keep you down. He wants you to enjoy abundance. The greatest thing about Jesus (God in human form) is that He wanted us to be able to do what he did and even more, and he left us his Spirit so that we, two thousand years later, are not without His power! It is amazing when we realize this, and learn to incessantly invite the Holy Spirit into everything. Amen.

To the best of my knowledge, the baptism of the Holy Spirit usually happens in a corporate environment. 'Where two or more are gathered...' It takes power to bring down power. After you are led to invite the Holy Spirit in your life, usually by a Spirit-filled leader, some of the signs of receiving a Holy Spirit baptism include but not limited to speaking in tongues, weeping or even laughing. These manifestations will also occur any time the Holy Spirit is welcomed into a meeting or a service. Once you receive the Spirit, you become sensitive to his authentic presence, or absence in everything. You can usually tell the presence of the Lord in a place by the changing of an atmosphere; an overflowing peace and a feeling of surrender. I have smiled, shouted, wept bitterly, or found myself praying in tongues and knowing those prayers were moving things in the spiritual realm.

Manifestations of the Holy Spirit's presence also happen in our day to day lives. He shows up in many forms: in words of wisdom before doing something; feeling uncomfortable about Godlessness; feeling uncomfortable with foul-mouthing, backbiting, gossiping, murmuring or lying. Friends, when the Holy Spirit fully dwells in you, there are certain attitudes and characteristics you just cannot keep. You can gauge your level of surrender to the Holy Spirit by your thoughts and actions towards others; your motivations for serving God and your level of integrity. Where the Spirit of the Lord is, there is freedom: people can be free around you; chains are broken, addictions and unyielding behaviours diminish, eyes are open such that people can begin to really know God through you.

When you have the Spirit of God, you also become sensitive to the enemy's presence and works. Do not take it for granted that the devil comes in many forms, many ways and in many things daily. This awareness though is not to bring fear, but rather confidence that Christ already defeated the enemy, and we have the Holy Spirit's power to follow suit. Make peace with that power. Go get your Holy Spirit baptism and *bienvenue au Kingdom of God!*

~

I recently read a book called 50 Scientifically Proven Ways to Be Persuasive. (Goldstein, N. J. et al. 2010). The book suggests that people's ability to understand the factors that affect their behaviour is surprisingly poor. Take a few minutes to ponder on the people and things that have influenced what you believe in. How do you respond to the word of God? What would meaningful experiences with God be to you?

Sometimes we quickly agree with the things we hear from the people and the situations surrounding us. It is my prayer that you would not be afraid to listen to God. Take a piece of paper and start writing all you feel about God, Jesus and the Holy Spirit; keep writing until it is clear. Then find your spot in the Kingdom of God...

CHAPTER 3: IT'S A MYSTERY

I thoroughly enjoy anything Victorian because I studied that era in Literature, and I love watching British adaptations of Shakespearean plays. That being said, I was vivaciously disturbed by Leonardo Di Caprio's attempt at Romeo; and it grieves me to admit that the brilliant Braveheart did not look right as Hamlet! The Americans did however act out a charming Shakespeare in Love. Gwyneth Paltrow won an award for the best actress in that 1998 movie. Her performance, albeit too sensual from a Godly standpoint, was poignant from a literary perspective. In Shakespeare in Love, which was not a Shakespearean play by the way, one of the clowns as it were, would habitually answer, 'It's a mystery,' when Shakespeare pondered on how the play was going to fall into place. Shakespeare in Love unimaginably portrays a William Shakespeare with writer's block. Imagine that.

"And without controversy great is the mystery of godliness: God was manifest in the flesh, justified in the Spirit, seen of angels, preached unto the Gentiles, believed on in the world, received up into glory." (I Timothy 3:13)

~

Life is a moving object, you may not see it now, but you will never come back to the old times. Live the life God has given you now, maximise its utility, now. If you are single now, you will not always have those free do nothing be yourself scream in the house days. Bask in the presence of God, for when you are married and with a family, responsibilities will demand more of your time. If you have a family, enjoy them, it will not be the same ten years from now. I reflected back on my life, my siblings and I were first kids living in the same house, then one sister got married and moved out, then we lost our parents, then I moved to North America. I left my family, friends, church and every familiar thing. My life here in Canada, is very different from my life in Zimbabwe. It makes me realize that life's motions do not allow us to hold on to what we've lived, but rather teach us how to use the lessons we have learned to navigate the new things God brings us to. We must therefore enjoy and appreciate our 'nows' and learn how to be fruitful in them.

Make your present life work for you as you move closer to the day God makes everything that has ever happened to you make sense.

God sometimes just does not make sense, but the scriptures encourage us to live each day; *"Holding the mystery of the faith in a pure conscience," (I Timothy 3: 9).* There are a great many rituals that believers adhere to; such as praying, reading the Word of God, fasting, tithing, restraint, humility, holiness and so forth. We as Christians believe there is power in the name of

Jesus. We believe that Jesus is the son of God, born of the Holy Spirit through a virgin; lived to conquer the devil, was crucified but on the third day resurrected and now sits on the right hand of God, interceding for every one of us as he won us back from death. That's all Christianity is about. You cannot make sense of it in the natural, it is absolutely spiritual. In Bishop Tudor Bismark's words, 'God does not want to be understood, but believed.' The mere idea of an invisible God can be baffling to the human mind. No human being can invent or manufacture another soul. We are created by a maker. The same maker is telling us;

"Lift up your eyes to the heavens, and look upon the earth beneath: for the heavens shall vanish away like smoke, and the earth shall wax old like a garment, and they that dwell therein shall die in like manner: but my salvation shall be forever, and my righteousness shall not be abolished. Hearken unto me, ye that know righteousness, the people in whose heart is my law; fear ye not the reproach of men, neither be ye afraid of their revilings [...] I, even I, am he that comforteth you: who art thou, that thou shouldest be afraid of a man that shall die, and of the son of man which shall be made as grass; And forgettest the Lord thy maker, that hath stretched forth the heavens, and laid the foundations of the earth..." Isaiah 51:6-7; 12-13a.

Chapters 18 to 24 in the gospel of Matthew discuss the return of Christ and the coming kingdom of God. I am looking forward to a new heaven and a new earth, meeting Jesus Christ, finally seeing God and reuniting with family and friends that have gone to be with the Lord already. I cannot wait to be done away with the earthly demands of this world and all the inequality. Millions are suffering, afflicted with sickness and disease. The inequality we have grown accustomed to and the man-made poverty in the poorest less developed countries is painful. Humans killing humans and children killing their own parents are common place stories. Surely all this has to come to an end. I want that day to come. Until then, we can pray as Paul did,

"Now the God of patience and consolation grant you to be likeminded one toward another according to Christ Jesus. That ye may with one mind and one mouth glorify God, even the Father of our Lord Jesus Christ." Romans 15:5-6

Let us return to the mystery.

"O the depth of the riches both of wisdom and knowledge of God! How unsearchable are his judgments, and his ways past finding out! For who hath known the mind of the Lord? Or who hath been his counsellor?" Romans 11:33

The mystery of the things of God is unlimited to say the least. There are times you get into a Sunday morning service and you can literally feel the devil suppressing people as the praise and worship is unmoving and you just feel like God's divine presence is not there. At such times a discerning pastor may ask the congregation to start praying and then the beauty of God's presence falls, demons flee, minds come back from distractions and just bask in the holiness of God. People then let go and begin worshipping God, or they regain ability to intercede. I like those moments. It is so sad that many Christians lack wisdom in using that gift, and also sad that many draw back from that power God's given us because they're uncomfortable in the manifestations of God's presence. The other side is folks who you know are not close to God or living out Christ-like character and come Sunday they start speaking in tongues using the Lord's gift in vain. Then the pastor who feels they have to perform holiness as opposed to trusting in Holiness- such as those who shout in tongues from their teeth; shake you and spit at you during the altar call and have the propensity to revel in falling bodies. The end result is detrimental to new believers becoming comfortable with the Holy Spirit.

Zeal for God is an amazing thing, and it is needful. But the line is so thin between sensationalizing spirituality and letting the Holy Spirit do all the work, not ourselves. My twenties have been crowned with displacement. I have moved continents, countries, and cities so many times and still feel like I am going to move again pretty soon. This has often left me, longing for my home church and the kind of worship I have experienced in Africa. I will tell you, Africans worship in such a distinct way, it is so easy for you to find God in Africa. In being exposed to different people, practices and places, I am realizing the work God is doing in me as I observe the way different people worship. I have been to a church where the praise and worship was amazing, the prayer time just after worship was phenomenal and the word was life changing. Then I have been to services where the message was so diplomatic and efficient, and the worship calm and soothing; and to services where children are given admirable attention. It's all been quite an experience. We all worship differently, and sometimes we all need worship in a different way. The most important thing to remember is to do it fervently, incessantly and to be fruitful. However you are worshiping, make sure you are reaching God each time, make sure you are producing fruit for God and make sure you are getting stronger each day. Most importantly, make sure you are teaching your children and making sure they will not forget the name of the Lord from the day they are born. God must be first place in your household. Pay attention to the women in the churches or cell groups. You will find many mothers who are strong Christians and serve in the church, but their hearts are sore for their children who have not yet come to Christ. They are now saved but their children are still in darkness. These women are so burdened watching their children erring and being callous towards such a precious salvation, yet having to deal with crumbling marriages, poor attitudes and unyielding children. Once a child comes to an age where they can make their own choices, it will become harder to start teaching them the commandments of

God – when they do not like anyone's rules! Many saved parents are left being very cautious about how to approach their adult children about Jesus. Do not let the enemy disempower you from raising a standard in your household. Let your children know where they come from; a sovereign God. I pray that parents will begin teaching our young about God, about Jesus, about sweet Holy Spirit; how to pray; how to fast for their schools and nations – to know that prayer is the backbone of their existence. If we can see a change in this area, many adults will be willingly akin to the things of God. Whatever the case, every breathing person can learn how to find the true heart of God.

What is the true heart of God? Is it in nailing every rule we believe God himself laid down for the faithful; is it okay for Christians to drink beer, to divorce, to tithe, to donate organs, to be rich or talk about material riches? There is a plethora of so-called Christian rules that seem to make Christianity conflicted. Many pre-Christians attack these areas, and many Christians themselves do not agree on many of them. For any doctrine, tradition or unclear practice, the best scriptural reference is probably Romans 14. In a nutshell, the chapter says, do not be about the business of justifying your eating meat, or not eating meat, worshipping on a particular day or not because really people who choose to eat meat or not, or worship on a certain day or not are doing it unto Christ- which is the important thing- as long as you're doing it unto the Lord. The key thing however, is not to perform your practices spitefully to offend your neighbour nor practice them in doubtful fear as that would downplay your faith. God's wish is simply for us to:

"[…] cleanse ourselves from all filthiness of the flesh and spirit, perfecting holiness in the fear of God." 2 Corinthians 7:1b

The rest believe it or not, shall be up to him:

"Who art thou that judgest another man's servant? To his own master he standeth or falleth. Yea, he shall be holden up: for God is able to make him stand." Romans 14:4

"So then every one of us shall give account of himself to God. Let us not therefore judge one another any more: but judge this rather, that no man put a stumbling block or an occasion to fall in his brother's way...Let not then your good be evil spoken of. For the kingdom of God is not meat and drink; but righteousness, and peace, and joy in the Holy Ghost ...Let us therefore follow after the things which make for peace, and things wherewith one may edify another." (Romans 14:12-13, 16, 19)

God gives us peace as well as part of the wisdom to discern between good and evil. Romans chapter 14:22 and 23b says

"Hast thou faith? Have it to thyself before God. Happy is he that condemneth not himself in that thing which he alloweth […] for whatsoever is not of faith is sin."

What these scriptures are saying is that gone are the days when the body of Christ needs to be fighting over rules, now is a time for power. We need power to heal the sick, raise the dead and help the lost come to Christ. God will convict the sinner who is doing wrong if this person is really searching for the truth. Now this certainly does not mean that if you see someone doing wrong, you turn a blind eye. Certainly not, rather, in love- you would help them as best you can and pray for the Spirit to reveal the truth to them, remember nothing is impossible with God. Ministers also have a particular framework that needs to be followed when there is wrongdoing in the church. We can no longer afford to be offended and ashamed about the things of God, this is who we are, for truly whose we are, is much greater than anything else.

Take a look at the following verse as Paul wrote to the church in Corinth:

"We then, as workers together with him, beseech you also that ye receive not the grace of God in vain. [...] Giving no offence in anything, that the ministry be not blamed: But in all things approving ourselves as the ministers of God, in much patience, in afflictions, in necessities, in distresses, in stripes, in imprisonments, in tumults, in labours, in watchings, in fastings; By pureness, by knowledge, by long suffering, by kindness, by the Holy Ghost, by love unfeigned, By the word of truth, by the power of God, by the armour of righteousness on the right hand and on the left, By honour and dishonour, by

evil report and good report: as deceivers, and yet true; As unknown, and yet well known; as dying, and, behold, we live; as chastened, and not killed; As sorrowful, yet always rejoicing; as poor, yet making many rich; as having nothing, and yet possessing all things."

Well that doesn't sound like fun...it's a mystery!

While we may never be able to answer all the questions to satisfaction, or win over all the doubting Thomases or learn to let others do what they do while we do what we do – people in the world are going to ask us Christians how and why we believe or do what we do. It's not a terribly bad thing to tug and haul on such issues - Peter the Rock did it;

"And he went into the synagogue, and spake boldly for the space of three months, disputing and persuading the things concerning the kingdom of God." Acts 19:8

So the body of Christ really needs to master the art of polemics if we are to win the hearts of those in bondage and may God help us.

"But sanctify the Lord God in your hearts: and be ready always to give an answer to every man that asketh you a reason of the hope that is in you with meekness and fear." 1 Peter 3:15

Tell God today, "Uphold me according unto thy word, that I may live: and let me not be ashamed of my hope." Psalm 116:116

Here's what God has to say about this mystery:

"Give thanks unto the Lord, call upon his name, make known his deeds among the people. Sing unto him, sing psalms unto him, talk ye of all his wondrous works. Glory ye in his holy name: let the heart of them rejoice that seek the Lord. Seek the Lord and his strength, seek his face continually. Remember his marvellous works that he hath done, his wonders, and the judgments of his mouth" I Chronicles 16:8-12

Isaiah 52 verse 1-3 shouts a cry: 'Awake O Zion, put on your strength, your beautiful garment of praise, and shake yourself from the dust!'

Praise God today you! Find strength in your praise, let your worship to God be the garment that beautifies you. When it seems no one else sees your worth and your beauty, God will. Let your love for God protect you and cover everything that you wish would just go away and become your past. God is majestic and he is faithful!

I am excited! God is about to do great things for many, and for you.

CHAPTER 4: MEET THE CORINTHIANS

The book of Corinthians unveils priceless
principles that can guide us today with our
Christian walk. Meet, the Corinthians...

~

*"For Christ sent me not to baptize, but to preach the
gospel: not with wisdom of words, lest the cross of Christ
should be made of none effect. For the preaching of the
cross is to them that perish foolishness; but unto us which
are saved it is the power of God." I Corinthians 1:17-18*

Those in the world may never understand the preaching
of the cross or the power of God, but we have to
maintain our understandings of the power of God.
The word of God further goes on to explain in verses
26-29 how God has chosen the foolish things of the
world to confound the wise.

*"And my speech and my preaching was not with
enticing words of man's wisdom, but in demonstration of
the Spirit and of power" I Corinthians 2:4*

However many times we fail to get through to people
because we tend to communicate the kingdom of God
erroneously, relying only on ourselves, our good words
and our own experiences. Paul tells the Corinthians;

"That your faith should not stand in the wisdom of men, but in the power of God. Howbeit we speak wisdom among them that are perfect: yet not the wisdom of this world, nor of the princes of this world, that come to nought: But we speak the wisdom of God in a mystery, even the hidden wisdom, which God ordained before the world unto our glory: Which none of the princes of this world knew: for had they known it, they would not have crucified the Lord of glory. But as it is written, Eye hath not seen, nor ear heard, neither have entered into the heart of man, the things which God hath prepared for them that love him. But God hath revealed them unto us by his Spirit: for the Spirit searcheth all things, yea, the deep things of God." 1 Corinthians 2:5-10. I love the clarity of the following verse:

"For what man knoweth the things of a man, save the spirit of man which is in him? Even so the things of God knoweth no man, but the Spirit of God." I Corinthians 2:11

Who can know the things of God, save the spirit of God Himself. We may never truly know what another person thinks of us, but in their hearts they know exactly how they feel about us. While we don't have power or access to the secret thoughts of a person, we have access to the secret things of God through the Holy Spirit. We need to get it, and keep it activated.

"But the natural man receiveth not the things of the Spirit of God: for they are foolishness unto him: neither can he know them, because they are spiritually discerned." (verse 14)

We have to recognize that it takes the anointing of the Holy Ghost for people to accept spiritual things. But that doesn't mean we are to put our own caps of righteousness and say, that's their own fate. See God is not like that, he wants his sheep saved rather than destroyed. We have a duty to pray for our brothers and sisters, for our communities and nations, for the Goth teenagers with a trillion piercings, for the good for nothing family members, for the co-worker with an attitude problem, for the spouse that hurts you or sees you as inadequate, and we have to do it faithfully…

"Let a man so account of us, as of the ministers of Christ, and stewards of the mysteries of God. Moreover it is required in stewards, that a man be found faithful." I Corinthians 4:1-2

When we know and truly understand what's coming ahead, we have to intentionally and somewhat competitively communicate the option people have. Yes people will call us names, try to avoid us, policies will be formulated to try silence us, co-workers will label us, sometimes we'll even go weary ourselves and just want to be 'normal.' Here's what Paul had to say about that: *"But with me it is a very small thing that I should be judged of you, or of man's judgment: yea, I judge not mine own self. For I know nothing by myself; yet am I not hereby justified: but he that judgeth me is the Lord. Therefore judge nothing before the time, until the Lord come, who both will bring to light the hidden things of darkness, and will make manifest the counsels of the*

hearts: and then shall every man have praise of God."
What a blessed assurance!

Here's another piece of Good News from Romans 3:3-4;

"For what if some did not believe? Shall their unbelief make the faith of God without effect. God forbid: yea let God be true, but every man a liar; as it is written, That thou mightest be justified in thy sayings, and mightest overcome when thou art judged."

May the body of Christ conquer in sharing the powerful message of the cross. We are advancing a kingdom! The door has been open for us to usher in righteousness as a mighty stream and prepare the way of the Messiah while forcing the world to reckon with us- effecting peace and prosperity. Again, give place to humility. In a culture that stresses self advancement, talent, and wherein it has become easily accessible for anyone to come up with an idea, patent it and sell it in a claim to show the "how to" of something- we tend to easily become high minded, puffed up and have proud looks. The Corinthians are reminded,

"And these things, brethren, I have in a figure transferred to myself and to Apollos for your sakes; that ye might learn in us not to think of men above that which is written, that no one of you be puffed up for one against another. For who maketh thee to differ from another? and what hast thou that thou didst not receive? Now if thou *didst receive it, why dost thou glory, as if thou hadst not received it?" I Corinthians 4:6-7*

Would it be fair then to say that Christians are meant to be the ever broken and ever reproached ones? Would it be fair to say that like their Father the Creator, Christians cannot be creative and have dominion over the things God endows them with? Not so, we are made in the image and likeness of God therefore it is innate for one who knows and confesses who they are in Christ to have a peculiar authority and a peculiar distinctiveness. The only difference between one who is in the world and one who is a child of God is the honour placed in every act. While the world will take lightly that what they have they have been given by someone mightier than they, Christians realize the grace of God in everything and handle their actions, words and convictions with honour to their Lord. The Kingdom of God is of a certain culture; one of purity, holiness, and peace. If you are battling with anything in your heart and if anything at all makes you uncomfortable and lose your peace, you should be weighing it against what God's word says about it. There is nothing wrong with goodness. The kingdom of God is such a one that the fullness of joy, of peace and of life is given, and we need to stretch out this kingdom. What most pre-Christians do not realize is how Christians simply long to share this good thing that's working for them. The opposite also happens; when Christians become endowed with knowledge of spiritual matters, they tend to forget the mandate to stretch out the empire by reaching out to people, and being there for one another. I will discuss at length the dynamics of human relationships pertaining to the kingdom of God later on in the book. Before I do that, I wanted to share on two utmost important things when spreading the kingdom: listening and giving.

Listening to someone is so important to building a relationship. I read somewhere how effective listening means when someone is relaying their concern to you; you are not being concerned for yourself by thinking of your response while they are talking to you. Often times we are not taking the time to listen to the stories of those who are lost. There is a reason why someone stopped believing in God, listen carefully and you will pick it up. There is a reason why someone thinks God is uncaring. There is a reason why someone is domineering. Instead of arguing or battering them about being Godly, sometimes we need to listen to their stories too, and love them for all they are and all they have been. One of the best ways to win someone's trust and loyalty, is by showing up in their lives when they need it most. Listen and care. After this has been done, giving is next. The word of God tells us how;

"Every man according as he purposeth in his heart, so let him give; not grudgingly, or of necessity; for God loveth a cheerful giver." 2 Corinthians 9:7

As with giving out your church offering, the first thing

is to purpose something in your heart, then give it cheerfully, not because you have to, but because it is your pleasure to give it. When you see someone else's need, you may not be able to wipe away all their tears, that is God's job, but you always hold power to make someone else's day better, with either your words, your time, your resources or your genuine love. What giving does according to 2 Corinthians 9:12-14 is this:

"For the administration of this service not only supplieth the want of the saints, but is abundant also by many thanksgivings unto God; whiles by the experiment of this ministration they glorify God for your professed subjection unto the gospel of Christ [...] and by their prayer for you, which long after you for the exceeding grace of God in you."

- it meets needs

- it causes thanksgiving to God

- and it confirms the righteousness of God in the giver and instigates the recipient to wish or pray a blessing on your life: giving causes people to pray.

Bless people, and they will pray for you. The covering of God on your life will be increased. Bless a sinner and he will bless God and be warmed up to believe God *is* good. Bless anyone and thanksgiving goes up to God, our saviour is glorified.

There are two key things we need to remember
in order to share the message of the Kingdom
in our generation: the truth must be revealed
and used, it is of a necessity; we must however
use all the wit in us to do so successfully.

~

When we communicate the Kingdom of God, there
are certain arts we have to master. I think of Jesus…

When the Jewish sectarian priests came to question
him over paying taxes to Caesar or over whose wife
one woman will be in heaven, he would start doodling
in the ground then respond to them in hypothetical
situations that exposed their own folly. When Simon
Peter under Satanic influence refutes Jesus' talk of
his forthcoming death, Christ rebuked the devil in
Peter's face. When his mother reprimanded him for
going off without parental guidance, he simply told
her he had to be in his Father's house. Upon being
requested to bow down to a golden image, Shadrach,
Meshach and Abednego answered back to a king, *"O
Nebuchadnezzar, we are not careful to answer thee in
this matter: If it be so, our God whom we serve is able to
deliver us from the burning fiery furnace, and he will deliver
us out of thine hand, o king. But if not, be it known unto*

thee, O king, that we will not serve thy gods, nor worship the golden image which thou hast set up." (Daniel 3:16-18.) What had to be said had to be said, and to God be the glory. See there will come a time in every believer's life where one has to defend their beliefs. We see it in presidential debates, in talk shows, in the streets, at school and at work. These are ideals like; Is there only one way to God, are homosexuals going to hell, suicide clinics should be legalized- church should not interfere in state business. In short, the world keeps shouting "religion" should know its place. How is it then, that we have a commandment to follow; *"Go ye therefore, and teach all nations, baptizing them in the name of the Father, and of the Son, and of the Holy Ghost: Teaching them to observe all things whatsoever I have commanded you: and, lo, I am with you always, even unto the end of the world. Amen." Matthew 28:19-20*

How I long to communicate God's love and faithfulness when I speak. One of my deepest desires is that God would make my words lucid and moving enough to make nations simply understand God's glory. Today I'd like to tell you, God's way is the right way. He is a sovereign and righteous God. Surely, when you have committed just to get a glimpse of him and seek him, he is faithful enough to answer your questions, still your doubts and give you grace to surrender the things you cannot understand. This generation will be won by miracles, signs and wonders. But for them to come and witness them in the first place, some foundation about the supernatural has to be communicated. It is imperative that the message of the cross be communicated. It is what it is. Yet we cannot afford to communicate the message of the Kingdom with self-glorifying motivations, but God-glorifying convictions. We ought not to be puffed up about a grace we ourselves were given;

"And these things, brethren, I have in a figure transferred to myself and to Apollos for your sakes; that ye might learn in us not to think of men above that which is written, that no one of you be puffed up for one against another. For who maketh thee to differ from another? and what hast thou that thou didst not receive? now if thou didst receive it, why dost thou glory, as if thou hadst not received it" I Corinthians 4:6-7

The next question becomes, with norms changing rapidly, and lines becoming dainty as to what is expected of Christians today; what "blue-prints" still work? While dated religious debates revolved around issues like eat sacrificed meat or not, women cover their hair or not, women preach or not; the questions our generation has include tithe or not, speak in tongues or not, preach on prosperity or not. Those in the world will challenge the notion of a man-woman model of marriage and defend homosexuality, find ultimate fulfillment with drunkenness and just simply not believe we are God's through Christ. How is it that the word of God written over twenty centuries ago remains relevant to us? I believe because the word is

God Himself. Anything that is of God is and will always remain holy. If we truly seek Him, we will find Him. He does want to lead us as sheep to the pasture, we have to believe and seek after the truth in Him. When we come to these peaceful and liberating revelations, we have a duty to share them. It has been thus far elusive for Christianity to pervade all aspects of life; we must now seek to teach the kingdom of God wittingly.

~

I love the word of God. All the guidelines, insights and words of revelation we need are in it. In 1 Corinthians 7 Paul discusses a number of issues the church in Corinth had been debating on all the way up to sexual relations between husband and wife- that sounds interesting- what he says in verse 5 is this,

"Defraud ye not one the other except it be with consent for a time, that ye may give yourselves to fasting and prayer; and come together again, that Satan tempt you not for your incontinency. But I speak this by permission, and not of commandment." Yes ladies and gentlemen, it was the bible that first advised married couples on keeping the sex-factor a top priority for a happy marriage. Notice how Paul talks about permission and commandment. Other times he uses phrases such as "judge in yourselves." (1 Corinthians 11:13) What I'd like to bring attention to is how the word of God says the saints of the Lord shall rule and judge the nations, we are to judge angels the bible says, we are made

in the likeness of the Creator himself- recall how Adam was given authority over every creature, he named every animal on earth. Hear this, we are not without the power to use sound judgment, we have all we need to address the grey areas of religion and the questionable things of humanity in our generation; because we are not without a helper; the precious Holy Spirit.

Some things Paul recommends by reason of sound judgment and the tried traditions, other things are direct commandments from God. Where the lines seem unclear or unaccounted for in the Bible, we have the Holy Spirit to show us the way as Christ promised. We are told whatever we do without faith will be counted as sin to us, and we are also told that of those practices that essentially don't steal away from the glory or power of God but others choose to follow, we are to let them be and not grieve our brothers for what they observe as an honour to the Lord. (I Corinthians 8: 4-13; I Corinthians 10:19-23) The book of Timothy also sheds remarkable light on how to handle the grey areas of Christianity as it applies in our generation.

"[...] that thou mightest charge some that they teach no other doctrine, Neither give heed to fables and endless genealogies, which minister [cause] questions, rather than godly edifying which is in faith: so do. Now the end of the commandment is charity out of a pure heart, and of a good conscience, and of faith unfeigned" I Timothy 1:3-5

If you find yourself caught up in dubious practice, or religious questions, it may be a good idea to ask yourself, is this debate or question instigating glory to God or not? Remember in Christ there is simplicity:

"But I fear, lest by any means, as the serpent beguiled Eve through his subtlety, so your minds should be corrupted [taken away from] the simplicity that is in Christ." 2 Corinthians 11:3

Here are a few other guidelines we find in scripture:

"This is a true saying, if a man desire the office of a bishop, he desireth a good work. A bishop then must be blameless, the husband of one wife, vigilant, sober, of good behaviour, given to hospitality, apt to teach; Not given to wine, no striker, not greedy of filthy lucre; but patient, not a brawler, not covetous; One that ruleth well his own house, having his children in subjection with all gravity; (For if a man know not how to rule his own house, how shall he take care of the church of God?) Not a novice, lest being lifted up with pride he fall into the condemnation of the devil. Moreover he must have a good report of them which are without; lest he fall into reproach and the snare of the devil. Likewise must the deacons be grave, not double-tongued, not given to much wine, not greedy of filthy lucre; Holding the mystery of the faith in a pure conscience.

"But continue thou in the things which thou hast learned and hast been assured of, knowing of whom thou hast learned them; And that from a child thou hast known the holy scriptures, which are able to make thee wise unto

salvation through faith which is in Christ Jesus. All scripture is given by inspiration of God, and is profitable for doctrine, for reproof, for correction, for instruction in righteousness." 2 Timothy 3:14-16

"In all things shewing thyself a pattern of good works: in doctrine shewing uncorruptness, gravity, sincerity, Sound speech, that cannot be condemned; that he that is of the contrary part may be ashamed, having no evil thing to say of you." Titus 2:7-8

"Finally, brethren, whatsoever things are true, whatsoever things are honest, whatsoever things are just, whatsoever things are pure, whatsoever things are lovely, whatsoever things are of good report; if there be any virtue, and if there be any praise, think on these things." Philippians 3:8.

(Read also 1 Corinthians 10:25-31 and Colossians 3).

Many things that are contested on this earth cause people to carry burdens. It could be issues surrounding the legalization of practices contrary to the word of God in relation to human rights; or issues that separate Christians themselves. Here I am writing this book trying to give my two cents on what I feel could work! Here is what 1 Corinthians 8:1 says,

"Now as touching things offered unto idols we know that we all have knowledge. Knowledge puffeth up, but charity [love] edifieth." In other words; "And if any man think that he knoweth any thing, he knoweth nothing yet

as he ought to know. But if any man love God, the same is known of him." I Corinthians 8:2-3.

We truly need to start making peace with everything God and give our all to loving God. As John Hagee once said, "If you love God the Father, the Son and the Spirit, you must also love the things of the Spirit." We ought to allow the spirit to take full control; we don't set the terms God does. Why because it's not about us!

"For we which live are always delivered unto death for Jesus' sake, that the life also of Jesus might be made manifest in our mortal flesh." 2 Corinthians 4: 11

The few minutes of awkward we have to endure as Christians will be nothing compared to the glory that awaits us when our team wins! Some of that weird stuff includes the powerful gift of tongues. Speaking in tongues is discussed at length in I Corinthians 14. What Paul was saying was paraphrased, speaking in tongues edifies you as a person because it confirms the Spirit of God working in you, and also it is the Spirit uttering and groaning on your behalf directly to God's spirit- good for you. Would be better if someone or yourself had the gift to interpret the tongues- and it is possible- when there's an interpreter, everybody gets blessed with God's word spoken. So he was saying, yes you've been arguing about speaking in tongues- understandable, but do not forbid speaking in tongues, rather do not abuse the gift or fail to make it produce fruit and also- it may not always be appropriate to be speaking in tongues in a gathering. Necessity and wit (discernment and wisdom) are needed to determine a time when strongholds have to be broken by praying in the spirit, which means praying in tongues. I will without a doubt attest to how beautifully I have felt the presence of God come down when my mind and my all give in to praying in the spirit. Spirit connecting with Spirit is beautiful, empowering and reassuring.

It is crucial to keep a clear conscience regarding the things of God because the enemy attempts to shake our faith in our minds. When we begin to ask the wrong questions and want to ascertain things according to human wisdom, or to glory for ourselves, we begin to doubt the truth and close the quietness open for the Spirit to do his work in us. Certainly many things we will never fully know or comprehend while on earth, that is the mystery of the faith, for He alone is God, we are not. Remember in the garden of Eden was a forbidden tree. As long as we are in the natural realm, there are things we simply cannot grasp until the perfect day when His glory is full revealed and every knee will bow every tongue confess that Christ is Lord. That day is surely coming, that is what we believe; this is why we believe. We wait and yearn for a kingdom of Holy, Holy, Holy; no more deaths, no more cancers and murders; no more poverty and evil. No more struggling in a world run by money, but being co-heirs with the King of Kings. We will live in an eternal state of complete peace, joy and happiness. Hallelujah! Everybody will be a singer as we all praise God together. I don't know what else is there, but I know it will be good. (Revelation 21)

There is something powerful about God himself, and loving Him. The first step in knowing what is expected of you in his kingdom is to love him earnestly, after that;

"For it is God which worketh in you both to will [want to do] and to do of his good pleasure." Philippians 2:13

~

The essence of having the Kingdom of God manifest in our generation is that we have to use our wit in declaring and defending what we believe.

~

So how exactly do we communicate? By the words we choose to speak, by the reactions we show in the workplace with family and friends, by how far we stretch our hands, by showing our commitments and yes by actively sharing the word of God, offering to share how what we believe in is working for us and by rebuking evil when we witness it. Sometimes we will talk to people face to face, but other times it's more effective when we write things down. Face to face interactions may sometimes come across as confrontational.

"Now I pray to God that ye do no evil; not that we should appear approved, but that ye should do that which is honest, [...] Therefore I write these things being absent, lest being present I should use sharpness, according to the power which the Lord hath given me to edification, and not to destruction." 2 Corinthians 13:7; 10,

"Study to show thyself approved unto God, a workman that needeth not to be ashamed, rightly dividing the word of truth. But shun profane and vain babblings: for they will increase unto more ungodliness. And their word will eat as doth a canker: of whom is Hymenaeus and Philetus; Who concerning the truth have erred, saying that the resurrection is past already; and overthrow the faith of some. Nevertheless the foundation of God standeth sure, having this seal, The Lord knoweth them that are his. And let every one that nameth the name of Christ depart from iniquity." I Timothy 2:15-19

"This know also, that in the last days perilous times shall come. For men shall be lovers of their own selves, covetous, boasters, proud, blasphemous, disobedient to parents, unthankful, unholy, Without natural affection, trucebreakers, false accusers, incontinent, fierce, despisers of those that are good, traitors, heady, high-minded, lovers of pleasures more than lovers of God; Having a form of godliness, but denying the power thereof: from such turn away...ever learning, and never able to come to the knowledge of the truth." I Timothy 3:1-7

I'll be honest sometimes as a Christian I feel good about myself that I have come to the truth and I look at how sinful or how nonchalant pre-Christians are and think, 'Man what has the world come to,' and move on. No child of God, do you think God is happy that his children are blinded and bounded by chains of the enemy? God would rather have the sinner repent and come to peace and joy, than to be in the bounds of sickness, sin, loneliness and spiritual death. I realized that I have been selfishly living in my own Christian world. My attitude has been, 'Well I know what's right and I do it. These other folk say they are not religious, how sad.' Period. How sad? The kind of heart Christ has for the lost is a heart of compassion, not callousness. The enemy has a mighty terrible rude awakening ahead, because he fell, he wants the world to fall too and God shamed. It is not enough to live in my little world doing my Christian duties. The kingdom of God was not selfishly created. Imagine if God said, well I want to keep just my immediate family for heaven! We need to pray for our cities, for our nations and for our communities. We need to pray for our co-workers, our neighbours and their children. When you're praying for a specific individual's salvation, desire to be a positive light in their life. Ask God to show you what he wants you to add to that life; how to do it and the confidence, wisdom and skill to do it. This verse in Ephesians brings out a lovely way to think about someone's salvation, and perhaps even a very powerful yet loving way to tell them of the Lord's desire to be Lord over their lives:

"That the God of our Lord Jesus Christ, the Father of glory, may give unto you the spirit of wisdom and revelation in the knowledge of him: The eyes of your understanding being enlightened; that ye may know what is the hope of his calling, and what the riches of the glory of his inheritance in the saints, And what is the exceeding greatness of his power to us-ward who believe, according to the working of his mighty power....vs 21 [which is] far above all principality, and power, and might, and dominion, and every name that is named, not only in this world, but also in that which is to come: And hath put all things under his feet, and gave him to be the head over all things to the church, which is his body, the fullness of him that filleth all in all." Ephesians 1:17-23

Father, teach me to love as you have loved...

I love spring for the soothing rain, the end of a long dreary winter season and looking forward to getting active outdoors. Spring smells heavenly fresh. The only thing I hate about it though, is worms (Forgive me Lord!) I'm getting chills just thinking about them.

~

"For this is the love of God, that we keep his commandments: and his commandments are not grievous." I John 5:3-4

We all have pet peeves or things we simply would rather not come to terms with. Believe it or not, it is much like a committed relationship with Christ. We all want to make it to heaven, be good people and be approved by God. However, we run into so many things about Christianity that we just cannot understand; other things we just dread and other things or people we do not necessarily like having to deal with. Let's call such things, spring worms.

Keeping your honour for God and constantly reaffirming him being the chief cornerstone of all our existence can be challenging. Before we tackle how to deal with the worms, perhaps it is not a bad idea to first remind ourselves why we even care in the first place:

"And not only so, but we also joy in God through our Lord Jesus Christ, by whom we have now received the atonement. Wherefore, as by one man (Adam) sin entered into the world, and death by sin; and so death passed upon all men [...] For if by one man's offence death reigned by one; much more they which receive abundance of grace and of the gift of righteousness shall reign in life by one, Jesus Christ. Therefore as by the offence of one judgment came upon all men to condemnation; even so by the righteousness of one the free gift came upon all men unto justification of life. For as by one man's disobedience many were made sinners, so by the obedience of one shall many be made righteous..." (Romans 5:11-12; 17-19)

"Knowing this that our old man is crucified with him, that the body of sin might be destroyed, that henceforth we should not serve sin. For he that is dead is freed from sin. Now if we be dead with Christ, we believe that we shall also live with him." (Romans 6:6)

"Likewise reckon ye also yourselves to be dead indeed unto sin, but alive unto God through Jesus Christ our Lord. Let not sin therefore reign in your mortal body, that ye should obey it in the lusts thereof." (Romans 6:11)

"Being then made free from sin, ye become the servants of righteousness." (Romans 6:18)

A common Shona expression goes; "It's as difficult as praying to God." Worshipping God does require unshakeable commitment. Amidst the joys of salvation also lie the "sacrifices of righteousness" [Psalm 4:5;

Dueteronomy 33:19]. So we find we do not always indulge in our fleshly wants, we commit to going to church regularly even when there's a big game playing or the weather looks dreadful, it means welcoming people into your house for prayer groups, fasting, abstaining from fornication, not watching certain things that could open the door to the enemy, constantly watching our tongues and letting God do the vengeance when we would rather serve justice to our emotions. Worshipping God means we have become servants of righteousness! Hallelujah!

The times we are living in are "testing times" for Christianity. More and more false and misleading doctrines are unfolding in the Church. We now find middle ground with the culture around us because the world's culture is prevailing faster than God culture. The bible says those that worship God must worship in spirit and in truth. Yet church is becoming louder than the instruction of the Spirit. I remember when I first went to spirit filled services, there were times when we'd just be silent after a worship song for time unending- basking in the quietness of the Spirit. Not rushing to put up a power point, not rushing for the speaker to start speaking, but letting the spirit of God move- waiting for as long as it took for it to move. Yet today, countless churches are shying away from manifestations of the presence of God- we feel awkward when people cry, raise hands, close their eyes, speak in a tongue or pray fervently.

How is it that we love God, and not love his Spirit when it comes down? How is it that we give our lives to Christ and feel we know how best he should control them?

Yes we are in a race with the world and we need to be on top as the body of Christ, but at what point do we stop trying to keep people entertained and engaged, and let the spirit of God himself move on them and tell them what he wants them to know? Let us remember; God is love, and oh how He loves us; but He is still God; sovereign, holy and to be feared. We are commanded not to be tossed by every wind of doctrine that comes, God is so much bigger- and many are failing to realize it. No jokes, no comfort zones, just truth and power. Take a look at this reminder in 2 Thessalonians 2: 2:

"That ye be not shaken in mind, or be troubled, neither by spirit, nor by word, [nor by letter as from us] as that the day of Christ is at hand. Let no man deceive you by any means: for that day shall not come except there come a falling away first, and that man of sin be revealed, the son of perdition; who opposeth and exalteth himself above all that is called God, or that is worshipped.....[...] vs 15, "Therefore, brethren, stand fast, and hold the traditions which ye have been taught, whether by word, or our epistle."

I pray you will never grow frail in the race. Now is such a time when the true sons and daughters of God shall be made manifest, we are now living in the times of the trying of our faith, I pray that God gives you the grace and power to win, and also the anointing to help many others win the race too. When confusion about biblical principles, spiritual things and God's expectations of us comes, it is worthwhile to remember the traditions, to be strong in prayer and to heed the spirit of the Lord as He leads you to *"Comfort your heart[s] and [e]stablish you in every good work." (2 Thessalonians 2:17).*

We tend to only see God as a loving Father, who loves everybody and loves us and takes care of us and loves us. In loving indeed our God loves us, but see also what the word of this same God cautions; *"That ye would walk worthy of God, who hath called you unto his kingdom and glory." (1 Thessalonians 2:12)* We do have a mandate to trust and obey- trust that God is real and loves us and has set us free, then obey what he would have us do. Walk worthy of God. Teach it to your children and your children's children that way we win the race. Remember we need to be careful not to lose the reward after we've fought the battle! We need to win to the end by loving God and obeying His word.

So said John - in the beginning was the word; which was from the beginning - with God. We come to learn that Jesus is this word. It should then follow that when we say we love Jesus, we should completely love the Word of God as it is, not in parts. To truly say Lord where you lead me I will follow, means stepping up and working harder to meet God's expectations of us wherever we are in life. Wherever I end up in life, I know He's leading me. So I have to be able to say, 'Send me, use me God, to do what YOU want, not what's in my head.'

This is how Paul lays it out to the Corinthians;

"Know ye not that the unrighteous shall not inherit the kingdom of God? Be not deceived: neither fornicators, nor idolaters, nor adulterers, nor effeminate, nor abusers of themselves with mankind, Nor thieves, nor covetous, nor drunkards, nor revilers, nor extortioners, shall inherit the kingdom of God. And such were some of you: but ye are washed, but ye are sanctified, but ye are justified in the name of the Lord Jesus, and by the Spirit of our God. All things are lawful unto me, but all things are not expedient: all things are lawful for me, but I will not be brought under the power of any. Meats for the belly, and the belly for meats: but God shall destroy both it and them. Now the body is not for fornication, but for the Lord; and the Lord for the body. And God hath both raised up the Lord, and will also raise up us by his own power. Know ye not that your bodies are the members of Christ? shall I then take the members of Christ, and make them the members of an harlot? God forbid. What? know ye not that he which is joined to an harlot is one body? for two, saith he, shall be one flesh. But he that is joined unto the Lord is one spirit. Flee fornication. Every sin that a man doeth is without the body; but he that committeth fornication sinneth against his own body. What? know ye not that your body is the temple of the Holy Ghost which is in you, which ye have of

God, and ye are not your own? For ye are bought with a price: therefore glorify God in your body, and in your spirit, which are God's." I Corinthians 6: 9-20

It is not the easiest thing to essentially ignore and separate yourself from the greater part of today's culture and norms. However, we come to a realization that there is something more than what revolves around us, and that thing is bigger, and that thing is the Kingdom of God. Reflect on the pride of having supported the New York Giants in 2012 or having always been an owner of a Macbook or an iphone before we lost Steve Jobs. You will see how we love identifying with what we hold dear. Reflect on the attention paid to immigration laws in any country and find out that we love our spaces, we love keeping our houses "ours" and then we mark our territories like animals. The kingdom of God is something like that. It is distinct too in certain ways. It has an open door policy- every living creature is welcome and wanted, but once you step in, you must be committed and step up to the standard of the Kingdom. When you hear about spiritual things, be able to say, "God you are doing something great!" as one writer put it. Cheer on Godliness, and have a strong commitment to God's kingdom: righteousness, peace and joy in the Holy Ghost.

People
Spring worms can also be other people. Sometimes

people are hard to deal with. They tend to be inconsiderate, overbearing, domineering, condescending, unkind, and the list is endless. Others just seem to constantly take out of you, while others seem to always leave you feeling less of yourself. Others are so easily offended and others quick to judge! People! You can probably remember a time when you said you don't ever want to have anything to do with a certain individual; we all relate to knowing someone we think has such an irreparable attitude. I'm sure we can all think of someone we prefer to steer away from. In my world of great ideas I once vowed it was possible to simply keep "such" people away from my life. Only when I stepped into the real world did I realize that I wasn't going to be alone in the kingdom of heaven! The task was not to always keep away from people who seemed to pull me down or just inconvenienced my life; the real task - was knowing how to respond to their choices. That "friend" who always seems to lie to you and use you, is there to sharpen your practice of boldness. You know they have stories, and they know it too, let them know you know! Then show them love; such a person will probably do something you wouldn't be able to do yourself and get you out of a rut one day. That co-worker who is gifted with natural talent, sharpness and confidence, but secretly intimidates you and they don't even love God…well there's something they can't do, these people are the easiest to minister to. The gossiper; the loud-mouth; the selfish worm; the bragger or the inconsistent friend? I cannot forget the person who hasn't really done anything to you but just annoys you for some reason. People sometimes have an envious spirit too. How many people have you met in life that are negative and never seem to bring you up or tell you how you are doing a great job - with sincerity - that is? I am almost certain we all have encountered the friend who always has a story of their own when you're recounting yours; or always reminds you of the bad side of the possibility. Such is the human spirit, treacherous and fickle.

As humans we have an unbelievable propensity to be generous yet selfish, and to be caring but inconsiderate. What is worse is that we may not even realize this. I am convinced that your core or birth family is the one unit that could sincerely wish you well. You can fight with your brother; not want to talk to them, think they're full of themselves, but *somehow you want* them to do well and you are happy when they overcome. Unfortunately it's not easy for many others to innately celebrate your accomplishments. People are always thinking, 'they're beating me to it.' How do you deal with the people around you? How do you deal with all their baggage and all they can potentially throw at you, while keeping yourself defined, and Christian? It's not easy. We need to ask God for wisdom to deal with people on a daily basis.

For the most part, we are either too nice to people to win their favour, or we're too callous towards them because we feel they don't deserve ours. Yet we have a perfect example in Christ who says to be the greatest you have to serve. Certainly Jesus was not a passive conformist, he was shrewd. He knew who questioned him to try and bait him, and he wasn't afraid to deal with those Sadducees and Pharisees. He would simply start drawing funny faces of them in the ground while beating them at their own folly, or remark how some things they just were never going to get! He could not always avoid them, but he dealt with their pride and their ignorance shrewdly. At the end of the day, the human being is lost on this earth. Allow people to show you their strengths, not just their weaknesses. In other words don't be too eager to realize and identify weaknesses, but likewise be eager to realize and celebrate strengths. You and I want to be celebrated, and so do about six billion other people and that's a lot of celebrating to do! We better start now. We have a desire to be witnessed. When you know someone with a tendency to talk about themselves often, it may be they simply have a need to be celebrated. There's nothing dreadfully wrong with that. In fact perchance many problems the world over are because we hardly celebrate others or listen, while everyone is just dying to be heard!

Learn how to witness someone else's happy moments, strong moments and victorious moments, and again, be able to say, "God you're doing something great." Remember His name has to be lifted up for the kingdom to come. Also let us be about the business of making the forgotten know they are not forgotten, and telling the so-called least, 'You're amazing.' Help somebody in your lifetime, pour into another's joy, celebrate with someone as if you were celebrating over yourself; that is faith. Dr Charles Swindoll puts it this way in a book I read, "How supportive are you of others' achievements?"

It might also be worthwhile to realize that forgiveness and not being easily offended plays a major role in reaching this kind of freedom. Forgiveness means letting go of past weaknesses and past faults and refraining from constantly bringing up the incident, especially when you want to justify yourself. We need to resemble God. The Lord does not say, "Well you know, I have dug you out of that lie you told Jack on the 5th of last month, and remember the adultery you committed with that woman, oh I don't know if I could listen to you right now!" God will for sure convict you when you sin the moment you do it. You will feel a certain heaviness and the Holy Spirit will withdraw from you. The emptiness that comes after is a mechanism he uses to show us that we cannot live without him, but in him is no darkness. He longs for us to realize our sinful nature, repent and run right back to him with a deeper longing to stay in him. Stay in the light of God, there is grief and heaviness in darkness.

A few years ago a 15 year old girl's testimony of heaven

and hell went viral. In an edited translation of her testimony, I read some things I knew but had not quite positioned in the ranks of importance. Forgive people you care about, forgive people that you could not care less about when they really rub you off the wrong way. Unforgiveness leads us to avert to love and compassion. Unforgiveness can lead to hell. Whenever spending time with God becomes stultifying, you must realize it is a demonic attack: there is a demon assigned by the enemy to specifically try to burn you out and cause you to curse God and die! These demons are real and are greedy to turn as many souls as possible away from the Creator. So next time you just don't feel like praying, or just can't, refuse to take it lightly and recognize the attack. It is an attack, so fight it. I know it is hard, I really do, but the best way to fight it is by spending time with God. Joyce Meyer put it simply in one sermon; you need to set aside time for God each day. Whether it is in the morning on the drive to work or school, at night just before bed, in the shower, at 5am, 3am or just before dinner with the family; your house needs God time. Your mind needs God time. It will help if you are specific and consistent about this time, aim for a target in your spiritual walk each month. When your commitment slackens make yourself accountable and noticeable. We easily get away with not fulfilling our commitments because we do not make them noticeable to others. When your child, spouse, pastor, roommate or friend know you to do a certain thing always, you become accountable because as humans we want to be deemed faithful to our commitments, capable and not lazy. One of my Facebook friends posted this once on their timeline, 'If it's important to you, you will make a way, if it's not you will find an excuse.' Quite profound I thought. No more excuses then, tame that flesh up!

Does this mean being Christian means being passive?

In traditional Christianity, forgiveness is prominently preached, and temperance and longsuffering strongly recommended. These values are fundamentals to the faith and often Christians are encouraged to exercise love above all things. How about the other side of the string; Christians who are difficult to show this kind of love to? If there is one thing that horribly throws me off, it would be inconsiderate Christians. Have you ever felt like there are some people you really try to love but they always cause you great disadvantage and emotional grief as well. Such as those who never really ask after you and always think you are obliged to be good to them but they hardly reciprocate? Or Christians who do not take the time to reflect on themselves but ignore the disadvantage they may be inflicting on others? Christians who basically have little co-existing etiquette for lack of a better term! Christians, be nice! Let's not take advantage of each other, let us genuinely care about each other.

When someone is going through something, pray with

them and remind them that if their situation continues you will love them and celebrate them regardless. Or maybe say something like, "I may not fully understand how you're feeling right now but I know God will lead you gently into the next reality of your life, I hope it will be an exciting one." "I pray that this season of your life will soon pass and that you will be victorious on every side, May God saturate you with grace and withhold no good thing. You are of sound judgement, wisdom and knowledge, and power to speak that everything in your life bow down to God's perfect will, and nothing else." Be sincere about it as well. Let your affection be genuine. When you listen to someone else's situation, genuinely feel for them, and genuinely desire to help. In our relations, we may have expectations of each other, we may have old wounds or current discontentment and trust me we all do, but the challenge is to be able to mutually and positively work on scraping out the differences. Believe in people's intentions. Be sensitive to what hurts another; what encourages them and what they are hopeful for. Remember your opinions valid as they may be, will without fail come across as positive or negative, and a person will always remember who believed in them and who didn't. When God needs to use your mouth, He will; when He asks you to do something for Him, your will needs to be subjected to His will. God being God, does not need our help to set a person straight!

The essence of true friendship whether in a family, in a

relationship or in the church is really the ability to have and feel freedom. Free in all respects to be ourselves, free to be happy, to talk and learn more about each other's interests, hopes, dreams, fears, strong points, weak points – and this kind of freedom comes with talking to each other honestly. When we are free and open towards each other we bring down the walls of unspoken bitterness, because we are free to confide in each other and truly want to build each other up. That is a clear conscience. True bliss is a clear conscience.

Give place to humility, to service and to considering another's feelings and hopes. So does it mean that Christians always have to suck up? Not to people, but to righteousness, peace and joy in the holy ghost- that's the Kingdom of God. Whatsoever things are good, whatsoever things are pure, whatsoever things are of good report- think on those things. Against such, there is no law.

If you are not a sold out believer of God the Father,
the Son and the Spirit, leave such people be!

"In the fear of the Lord is strong confidence." Proverbs
14:26

~

Some of the best demonstrations of the kingdom of
God manifesting are in the book of Acts. In chapter 1
we encounter the day of Pentecost and word spreads
quickly that the Galileans are speaking in diverse
tongues much to the vexation of the Jews. Doubt
crept in and very commonly to men, when they do
not understand something they will fortify their own
insecurities by speaking out their unbelief. One only
needs to read youtube comments on literally anything
to understand this. As the story unfolds in 2:13 they
start mocking the believers, "These men are full of
wine." Do you know what Peter did when he heard
the reverent name of Almighty God being alluded to
as drunkenness?

*"But Peter standing up with the eleven lifted up his
voice, and said unto them, 'Ye men of Judaea, and all
ye that dwell at Jerusalem, be this known unto you, and*

hearken to my words: For these are not drunken, as ye suppose, seeing it is but the third hour of the day. But this is that which was spoken by the prophet Joel…" Acts 2:14-16

From verses 17-28 Peter recites Joel's prophecy as it is, demonstrating indisputable knowledge of history and the word of God. He reminds them of David and explains the scriptures, showing how every prophetic word they were familiar with echoed the advent of their own saviour Christ whom they failed to recognize. Man oh man, how we need knowledge! After Peter had finished admonishing the Jews with unfeigned scripture and the boldness of the Lord guess what it did to them?

"Now when they heard this, they were pricked in their heart, and said unto Peter and to the rest of the apostles, Men and brethren, what shall we do?" Acts 2:37

See as witnesses to the kingdom we need to know how to explain our Lord to our audience at the time. The Jews misunderstood Jesus' kingship and crucified him. Today's generation has side-lined Jesus and disregards him as cornerstone of their lives. We need to make the world understand what they have done and prove how Christ was and still is. I like one of Windsor Christian Fellowship's visions: to be relevant to the culture we live in. It is their mandate that Christ be not ignored in our generation. Are people empty inside? Are their relationships breaking down fast, are they frustrated and angry with their lives, work, the environment, their governments, corporate greed, poverty and sickness? Such are the lives of those living without the chief cornerstone to hold everything together and reigning on their behalf. The word of God says perfect peace will he give them whose minds are stayed on him; nothing shall offend the righteous the book of Psalms says; when news of disaster strikes the righteous need not fret and no good thing will He withhold from them that love him.

"[A good man] shall not be afraid of evil tidings; his heart is fixed trusting in the Lord." Psalm 112:7

"Great peace have they which love thy law: and nothing shall offend them." Psalm 119:165

Instead of making much ado about the kingdom of God, we have mastered the arts of fighting for fundamental rights and freedoms but quieted the Spirit of God. May the Lord be lifted up in all the earth.

Note also how it was the Jews that came to Peter and the apostles while they were about the business of doing God's work- gathering, teaching and ministering. I once had a lovely conversation with a close friend of mine. She was telling me how their twelve year old son was getting baptised and her family was officially becoming members of their church. She is Indian and migrated to Canada several years back, so as she was retelling her story she was also reinforcing her comfort with the decision her family had just taken to be a part of a church with a worship style much different from her culture's. However what really attracted me was how at this new church they hosted car shows, sports tournaments, offered free ESL classes and offered free entry into their church gym to outsiders. What an amazing and unselfish way to minister to others. Many of the people this church touches have ultimately developed a loyalty to the church and fallen in love with Christ. As Christians we have tended to keep outsiders different and secluded from us, we talk about having them come but the programs we construct to win the lost are tailored to touch those who have already made the first step or are already somewhat comfortable with the notion of entering the doors of a church.

In chapter three we are taught the lesson to be quick to applaud the Prince of Life. I often rue at the many times I could have impressed upon the heart of a co-worker or stranger by simply saying, "My Jesus is really giving me a great day," or the familiar, "I'm too blessed to be stressed!" Make it a habit to say, "Man God loves me!" or "I know God will make things better for me." Sometimes all it takes for someone else to start believing and seeking the hand of God in their lives is just hearing someone else say it's working for them. In Acts chapter three Peter and John spoke healing into a lame man whom everyone knew all his life as a lame beggar- nothing new. People could not believe it, they were sore amazed! Imagine being in a situation where you have changed something that everyone else had struggled with for years? Imagine being the one being talked about as the guy who could do it- When Peter realized what was going on he quickly and resolutely admonished,

"Ye men of Israel, why marvel ye at this? Or why look ye so earnestly on us as though by our own power or holiness we had made this man to walk? The God of Abraham, and of Isaac, and of Jacob, the God of our fathers hath glorified his Son Jesus, whom ye delivered up; and denied him in the presence of Pilate, when he was determined to let him go. But ye denied the Holy One and the Just and desired a murderer to be granted unto you."

Wow. There's one way of doing it. When a co-worker asks you how you manage to cope with a difficult situation, without complaining about anything and staying up-beat, realize it as an opportunity to declare, "The same faith that many avert from is exactly what keeps me this great, God has a great impact on my attitude." Are we too terrified to say such words, when it is the truth? Are we too often choosing to save face and be accepted by the world that hates us, rather than giving God all the glory? Lift up your countenance child of God; no person has the fundamental right to condemn you for how you choose to explain your happiness. Fear not. Indeed the world will attack the God who made her, using man-made laws. We are told of this in Acts 4 verse 18:

"And they called them, and commanded them not to speak at all nor teach in the name of Jesus. But Peter and John answered and said unto them, Whether it be right in the sight of God to hearken unto you more than unto God, judge ye."

I call Peter and John's response wisdom, shrewdness, wit, single-mindedness and confidence. It reminds me of Shadrach, Meshach and Abednego upon being commanded by King Nebuchadnezzar to worship his golden image;

"O Nebuchadnezzar, we are not careful to answer thee in this matter, If it be so, our God whom we serve is able to deliver us from the burning fiery furnace, and he will deliver us out of thine hand, O king. But if not, be it known unto thee, O king, that we will not serve thy gods, nor worship the golden image which thou hast set up." Daniel 3:16-18

Yes, when a despot is challenged and publicly emasculated, many will have to contend with his wounded pride-the Judaean three-all got the death penalty! That thought truly causes shivers down many pre-Christians and un-serving Christians' spines. Somewhere down the road we were told that once we decide to do great things for God, greater tribulations will attack us. We do not want to hear that! However if you lose self for Christ, he will surely reward, protect and avenge you. Take a look at how the condemned guilty walked 'death'-free;

"there was not a single hair singed nor did the smell of fire pass on them and that same Nebuchadnezzar said, Blessed be the God of Shadrach, Meshach and Abednego and ordered that anyone who spoke against their God be cut in pieces and their houses made a dunghill." Daniel 3:27

The apostles certainly realized the dangers and risks of proclaiming the saviour. So they prayed specifically: *"And now, Lord, behold their threatenings: and grant unto thy servants, that with all boldness they may speak thy word; By stretching forth thine hand to heal; and that signs and wonders may be done by the name of thy holy child Jesus." Acts 4:29-30.* Every day when we step out into the world, we need to ask our Father for strength and power to proclaim Jesus and ask that he would back us up! There are times when I ask God not to let his healing power to be less spoken of; for him to be jealous with my joy and to restore to me the joy of salvation for indeed sometimes it is tough to be a believer. At times we need to ask God to show us again that we can have joy and happiness as a born again. In desperation, I've often prayed as though I were reminding God he has the power. We have to keep our minds and bodies ever ready to push in the spirit, when you push you're merely believing so hard with your mind, soul and strength and fighting the enemy by denouncing doubt and proclaiming God is greater! That is faith, and that's what God wants to see from us.

In singleness of mind Peter and the apostles carried

on speaking about Christ, hearing from the Spirit and uttering things in His name; causing healings and deliverances. They were thrown into prison but the angel of the Lord came and opened the prison doors. The angel told them, *"Go, stand and speak in the temple to the people all the words of this life." Acts 5:20.* Whatever will stir up someone else's faith in God, you need to be sharing.

Stephen
Before the stoning and Jesus standing up for him, Stephen *"full of faith and power, did great wonders and miracles among the people [...] and they were not able to resist the wisdom and the spirit by which he spoke." Acts 6:8;10*

May the grace of God and his spirit be upon you greatly such that the people that hear you will not be able to resist His Spirit in you.

Simon the sorcerer
The apostles' journey continues, Samaria receives the word of God and falls to the kingdom. However there is a peculiar man in Acts 8:9. A cunning sorcerer with a flourishing reputation; bewitching the people of Samaria and everyone has an inflicted fear of him. Peter and John are sent down to Samaria to strengthen the newly acquired territory. These people had accepted Jesus as Lord and Saviour but had not yet received the baptism of the Spirit (vs 16). They were saved, but did

not avail much; Christians at heart, but unlike their new father. The apostles hence waste no time and begin laying hands imparting the power of the Holy Ghost. Alas the sorcerer sees this, and covets that kind of power so he makes an offer; money. Imagine someone offering you money for the gift of God you possess in this free market economy we are living in. You think copyright then patent- returns and economies of scale once your 'product' hits international markets and has links on social networking sites and is recommended by a talk show host. If you have foresight, you would also look up a good lawyer who would help you file lawsuits against any plagiarised use of your new *How to possess God's power* book. Once reviews go up about how well your product is working, you are on top of the list for conference speakers, so of course it would follow that you would demand premium suite hotel accommodation, business class tickets and an honorarium surely not less than 10K. Your gift is unique.

Child of God, *"Let your moderation be known unto all men. The Lord is at hand." (Philippians 4:5)* Peter reprimands Simon the sorcerer vehemently, *"Thy money perish with thee because thou hast thought that the gift of God may be purchased with money. Thou hast neither part nor lot in this matter: for thy heart is not right in the sight of God."* The kingdom of God is higher above money. While the world we are living in is about investing in and securing the future, the kingdom of God shall be an inheritance guaranteed only by grace, through the Son by the Spirit. As we yet live in this world may the Lord give us hearts that long for the kingdom; that as battalions will go to war for their crowns and countries, we will defend the righteousness of the Kingdom of God.

The Ethiopian Eunuch

Before Ethiopia's great famine that inspired Michael Jackson and fellow artists to sing, 'Heal the world,' Ethiopia was the richest country in the world and was ruled by a woman!

Acts 8:27- A man of Ethiopia, an eunuch of great authority under Candace queen of the Ethiopians, who had the charge of all her treasure, had come to Jerusalem to worship. This man was sitting reading the book of Isaiah in his chariot when God's spirit told Philip to go to this chariot. Philip quickly obeys. When he meets this eunuch he asks, 'Do you understand the word of God?' I am wondering the reaction of an un-religious person if asked that same question. The eunuch responds, 'Actually no, I need help.' The word of God in verse 31 tells us "he said 'How can I except some man should guide me?' And he desired Philip that he would come up and sit with him."

Father may you give lost souls great desire to hear your word and know your spirit.

This un-named eunuch hears Philip out, is introduced to Christ and asks to be baptized! How amazing! The key thing in this story is the eunuch's position. He was a man of great authority under the queen and in charge of the government coffers. Would it not be a marvellous thing to have our federal governments' chief economists and governors want to know God's plan and align with it? If men and women in authority refused to be used by the enemy for earthly gains, and instead rejoiced in the promises and commandments of God. God wants them to, and many are hungry and desire to stand for the principles of God but the dark principalities of this world have them tied down. Many men in high places do not know where to go and have fewer chances of anointed men and women of God going to them to say, 'Let me tell you what Jesus' power can do for you.' May we remember to pray for their souls. May God open up more doors of ministration to those in decision making positions. May we give in more to God than to our desires, may we hunger more for love from God than for love from people. May we come to realize that the Lord does not expect things from us and out of us that we cannot do. He has given us his righteousness so it *is* within our capabilities. Amen.

A Lady Named Dorcas

This woman was "full of good works and almsdeeds which she did." (Acts 9:36) Dorcas, commonly known as Tabitha, dies. When word comes that Peter who had been doing mighty exploits was near Joppa, where Dorcas had died, he is quickly summoned. All the widows Dorcas had helped stood in agreement trusting Jesus could raise her from the dead. Peter prayed – Dorcas was raised from the dead – many in Joppa got saved...because of a lady called Dorcas. Godly folk, help out all folk. The kingdom of God has no lack, always realize the power you have to help anyone in need. A meal, a cheque, a smile, a prayer, a kind word, a good attitude, a shoulder to cry on, confidentiality, an encouragement, a place to stay - the list is endless.

Call the Christ to Join Godly-folks today!

The story begins in Matthew 21. It is Palm Sunday, biblically known as the Triumphant Entry, the first significant event under-toning Christ's death. Jesus enters Jerusalem meekly upon a colt and majestically the multitudes herald him laying their garments and palm leaves before him, singing, 'Hosanna in the highest!' Then almost suddenly the jubilee is cut off upon entering the temple of God in the Holy City only to find traders and money-changers doing business in the house of God. Christ condemns, "My house shall be called the house of prayer; but ye have made it a den of thieves!" In the Easter movies, this is the part we see an angry Jesus, doves aflying and tables turning. When we divert the use of a sanctuary and it becomes less of a house of prayer, we rob God of honour. We are thieves.

After the reprimand Christ sets right to work- healing the lame and opening the eyes of the blind. Children start praising and chief priests get 'sore displeased.' They confront him, "Hearest thou what these say?" I thought to myself how many times Christians get confronted with subtle accusations or ingenuine probes about biblical principles; 'Are you saying that my son is a sinner because he is gay?' 'Are you saying that there is only one way to God?' Quite simply Christ responds back, "Yea; have ye never read, Out of the mouth of babes and sucklings thou hast perfected praise?" And he left them...

Sometimes you need to speak up for your convictions, speak up for your faith then leave. It is not due for us to shove our beliefs down anyone's throat. It is our obligation to share it, if accepted God be praised, if not yes sometimes we have to shake the dust off and go. When people try to make you question your faith in Christ, they are sadly stealing from his glory, and stealing from your boldness. The Holy Spirit will guide us and impress on us to share more with someone ready for the truth. When we go out into the world to reach the lost, it's not just nice lost people we will encounter, we are sent out among wolves. Until a person is willing to come to Christ, they will not. As we are led, and other times with only wisdom and boldness can we minister the love of Christ to another. Do not waste time with arguers and men with hearts of stone. The word of God in Zechariah 7:13 says;

"But they refused to hearken and pulled away the shoulder, and strapped their ears, that they should not hear. Yea, they made their hearts as an adamant stone, lest they should hear the law, and the words which the Lord of hosts hath sent in his spirit by the former prophets."

Don't allow the enemy to steal your rights as a Christian; don't let the world steal what you have been freely given. Do not allow the enemy to steal the joy of your salvation. You are saved, shout it loud! Do not keep your mind on the words and views of non-believers, keep your mind stayed on God. This too shall pass, as God tells us;

"And I will multiply the fruit of the tree, and the increase of the field, that ye shall receive no more reproach of famine among the heathen..." Ezekiel 36:30

In truth God has put a measure of faith in each one of us, scripture says; *"He hath shown thee o man, what is good; and what doth the Lord require of thee, but to do justly, and to love mercy, and to walk humbly with thy God?" Micah 6:8*

FAITH...

And then he was hungry, but the fig tree had nothing to offer him, he curses it in staunch authority. The disciples are awed and Jesus answers, *"If ye have faith [...] you will move mountains. And all things, whatsoever ye shall ask in prayer, believing, ye shall receive." (Matthew 21:21-22)*

All you need lies in your ability to believe God can do all things. Not just one thing, but that God can do all things, for indeed all power belongs to God. The Psalmist says, *"God hath spoken once; twice have I heard this; that power belongeth unto God." (Psalm 62:11)* I like to put in "all power," not curses, not the devil, not the world systems. Power belongs to our God!

And so they begin to question him, the Christ. By what authority doest thou these things? (vs 24) Jesus answers, "I will also ask you one thing, which if ye tell me, I will tell you by what authority I do what I do. The baptism of John, whence was it? From heaven, or of men?" The scribes and Pharisees reason, realizing he had put them in a corner. "We cannot tell" they mutter. In lay man's terms, Christ says to them, 'Well then, neither will I tell you by what authority I do what I do,' and proceeds to speak in parables that exposed their ignorance.

If we would dare to have faith for God to move in our lives miraculously and wonderfully, should it also not follow that we would likewise defend the faith we have in Him?

Only that we need wisdom and boldness to do it. We have perfect templates in the word of God from the man who lost faith while walking on water and denied Christ three times in his face. Peter, who was described as the rock by Christ himself, utters these words:

"It was necessary that the word of God should first have been spoken to you: but seeing ye put it from you, and judge yourselves unworthy of everlasting life [lo, we turn to the Gentiles.]" Acts 13:46

"Whether it be right in the sight of God to hearken unto you more than unto God, judge ye." Acts 4:19

"For what if some did not believe? shall their unbelief make the faith of God without effect?" Romans 3:3

Believers, even in the midst of an unbelieving generation, God is greater. If you have already made that decision in your life to follow Christ with all you have, wonderful and God be praised for you. If you are still on the borderline and have your reservations, may God's spirit not let you go until you have found peace with His Spirit. If you are a pastor or a leader in a church, do not choose how to describe the Son of God! Teach how to know Him. Remember John the Baptist? He was the fore-runner of the Christ, the greatest prophet; the man who baptized the son of God. That mighty John suffered persecution and was imprisoned for his beliefs, yet his expectations of this Jesus he preached about were not met. John sends his disciples to go ask, 'Are you that messiah or should we look for another.' Do you know what Christ tells them;

'the blind receive their sight, the lame walk, the lepers are cleansed and the deaf hear, the dead are raised up and the poor have the gospel preached to them…'

It is the verse that follows that I really wanted to bring attention to as it resonates shockingly with our generation:

"And blessed is he, whosoever shall not be offended in me." (Matthew 11: 1-6)

If you are just starting your spiritual walk, or you are on the borderline, my word of encouragement to you is do not be offended in Christ. Jesus is such a good guy. If you have been a Christian all your life, but have not allowed the Holy Spirit to move mightily in your life, I urge you, do not be offended in Christ. It is astounding how many churches have quenched the Spirit, forbidden or neglected speaking in tongues, dancing in the joy of the holy ghost, praying for healing, casting out demons and believing for great revival. We get uncomfortable with the manifestations of God's spirit just as John the Baptist was getting uneasy with the way Jesus was handling his Messiahship. Christ is saying to you today, blessed are you if you will not be offended in me. It is truly sad how even when it is not working in bringing the lost in, the church continues to preach endless stories of Jesus loving little children, how he died for us, how he said give to the poor and to have compassion but not about his power. For whatever reason, churches and families hardly talk of how the same Jesus also said all manner of sin would be forgiven except when people speak against the Holy Spirit (Matthew 12:31-32.) We are omitting the story of Christ lamenting over the cities that did not repent, Chorazin, Bethsaida and Capernaum (Matt 11:20-24). We are forgetting all that has been said about Christ, and how he actually has commissioned us to do greater things than he. For the kingdom of God is not in words, but in power! This lie from the enemy is two-sided, believers who do not use the power of the Holy Spirit, and believers who abuse the power (gifts) of the Holy Spirit. Such as those are self-glorying evangelists and ministers with a gift of healing who need money for some holy water or a healing cloth, build luscious buildings without God's approval and are forced into dubious means to fund and maintain them. Such raises my eyebrows too, however the answer to that is reprimanding such lack of wisdom, not shutting the door to the things of the Spirit! If a church is educated on the Holy Spirit and the power of God, moves of the Holy Spirit will bless everyone present. When you are in a Holy Spirit filled atmosphere, you will know if it is truly God because His word assures us, 'My sheep know my voice,' and wherever the Spirit of the Lord is, there is liberty. If you are truly hungry and open to the things of God, you will not be offended by the way He acts out His Sovereignty.

Faith is also expressed by the forgiveness phenomenon. We believe that by virtue of being born after Adam, we are sinners because he sinned, but Christ came so that he would pay for all the sin we would commit as long as we confess and believe in him being the Son of and only way back to God. Now as we have been forgiven, we are also expected to forgive one another. This is not always easy as we will always remember who hurt us. Forgiveness therefore does not mean pretending that we were not hurt; it means we cease to talk about past hurts and we do not perpetually hold it against the perpetrators. You can consciously choose not to talk about what happened to you, and thereby not glorify a bad act, a bad decision made by a fellow human. Remember only God deserves all glory. Rather, thank

God that He is able to make the person that slighted you a better person, claim them into the kingdom if they are not believers, tell the devil that he has to let go of God's children. This is what faith is about.

In the book of Galatians we learn about the fruits of the Spirit such as love, joy, peace and longsuffering. We can only bear fruit that we have planted. This implies that we are not suddenly going to have love, joy, peace and patience; we have to cultivate them. Tell yourself, 'I need to seek after joy and to reflect joy in my life.' We need to learn how to find peace. Peace with one another and peace in trying times. When everything is going wrong in your life, where is your peace? Find it. Equally important is the ability to be patient. Patient about your hearts desires, patient about meeting that person, about your financial breakthrough, patient about your idea to generate residual income. Being patient means that we stop muttering and emphasizing on how long we've been waiting or how much you want this thing; God knows you are believing for it, so it is needless for us to be telling people over and over how long we have been waiting. When you share your desire, make sure you are sharing to edify yourself or the other person. As much as you can, do not open your mouth to mutter your disgruntlement because God will surely count it as doubt and unbelief. We have to learn patience and this may mean saying, "God this is really hard, but I am going to trust you are in control. You have plans to bring me every good thing, so I would rather have your will come quick than my own plans."

All this "Christian-stuff" may all seem a little too much for you, perhaps over-rated or just too esoteric. Yet to God, it is his all, his creation stolen away in deceit and He wants us back...

We are so important to God that he has called us His temples. If you read the bible, the theme of the temple is rampant and there is deep meaning to it. Let's have a look at some of these themes. It generally starts with Moses. After spending forty days and nights listening to the voice of God in Mount Sinai, Moses reiterated to the Israelites how God's tabernacle (temple) had to be made:

"And they came, both men and women, as many as were willing hearted [emphasis added] and brought bracelets, and earrings, and rings, and tablets, all jewels of gold: and every man that offered offered an offering of gold unto the Lord." Exodus 35:22.

A lot more was brought in for the building and it was the best. The first thing to note here is how Moses did not force anyone, the bible says as many as were willing hearted. For something good to be established, a good foundation has to be laid. Grumbling spirits and partially willing hearts cannot partake of the Lord's plan in full. In your household, make sure that a temple is established, catch your children while they are young.

The temple of Moses had the finest detail. The curtains were of 'fine twined linen' with beautiful loops at the edges and joined together with gold. One of the wise men; Bezaleel, made the ark of wood, which was two and a half cubits long, and a cubit and a half wide. (A cubit being the size of the length between the wrist and the elbow.) The ark was overlaid with pure gold within and without, had fine linen of blue, purple and scarlet was used for the cloths and the curtains. It was a marvellous work to say the least and the detailed description of this occupies Exodus chapters 36 to 39. But here is the good news: *"Know ye not that ye are the temple of God, and that the Spirit of God dwelleth in you? [...] for the temple of God is holy, which temple ye are. I Corinthians 3:16-17.*

If you want to get a head start at being super spiritual, that right there would be a good time to shout, "Glory!" and start speaking in tongues, am I pushing it? Worth a try!

"And what agreement hath the temple of God with idols? For ye are the temple of the living God; as God hath said, I will dwell in them; and I will be their God, and they shall be my people." 2 Corinthians 6:16

This is how God sees you. He has called you His temple, made of pure gold. The temple in Jerusalem took forty-six years to be built, imagine how detailed and immaculate it was. Have you ever realized how detailed your body is; every cell, artery, ligament and organ? The same beauty that is evident in ancient buildings and in a healthy human body, is similar to how God wants your spirit man to be. God sees you as a spectacular being. You are definitely not a physical temple, your body may not be very co-operative right now, but do you realize that you have been given the power to make your spiritual being as powerful and wholesome as can be? How, because the spirit of God dwells in you, so you have the sovereign right not to accept unworthy habits, talk, company and materials into your life. Say no to things that stain your royalty, say no to things that make the spirit of God not feel at home in you! Your spiritual growth can have humble beginnings, it may start as small as a mustard seed, but that seed will grow. All you need is to sow the seed. The seed principle also works when you wish someone else would get saved. You may not be able to get someone to receive Christ into their heart when you first share the message of Christ, but that small mustard seed you sow may one day grow into a flourishing tree of righteousness, grounded in Christ. God will give you wisdom and understanding of the things of the kingdom:

"Then wrought Bezaleel and Aholiab, and every wise hearted man, in whom the Lord put wisdom and understanding to know how to work all manner of work for the service of the sanctuary, according to all that the Lord had commanded." Exodus 36:1

You are God's temple, so God is going to make sure

he builds you up excellently. It is no mistake that you come from the family, nation or continent you are from. It doesn't matter who your father is or what he has done. You have a throne to co-inherit. Too many a time we take it lightly that we are a part of God's plan and neglect our lineage in Christ. When Jesus went missing from his parents at the age of twelve, he was found in the temple. While his parents could not fathom why he did something terribly irresponsible like that, he was stunned at their failure to realize his need to be in the house of the Lord. Christ today still yearns to be in the Lord's temple...in you! He loves being in you, but he wants no sheep, cattle, pigeon-trading and gambling in his house! No thieves, just faith!

It is my prayer that you would be ready and found approved when Christ returns; for many are called, but few are chosen. I pray that you would run the race and not get weary. Give it your all to defend the kingdom of God, for this kingdom belongs to one such as you.

"Hearken unto me, ye that know righteousness, the people in whose heart is my law; fear ye not the reproach of men, neither be ye afraid of their revilings. For the moth shall eat them up like a garment, and the worm shall eat them like wool: but my righteousness shall be forever, and my salvation from generation to generation." Isaiah 51:7-8.

"For the earth shall be filled with the knowledge of the glory of the Lord, as the waters cover the sea." Habukkuk 2:14

A secular person can be described as one who consciously and constantly decides not to feel anything for God. Getting together with others on the basis of Christianity is not a part of their lives; their car music does not include worship, and conversations at home dare not involve God.

"The Lord is not slack concerning his promise, as some men count slackness; but is longsuffering to us-ward, not willing that any should perish, but that all should come to repentance. But the day of the Lord will come as a thief in the night; in the which the heavens shall pass away with a great noise, and the elements shall melt with fervent heat, the earth also and the works that are therein shall be burned up. Seeing then that all these things shall be dissolved, what manner of persons ought ye to be in all holy conversation and godliness, Looking for and hasting

unto the coming of the day of God, wherein the heavens being on fire shall be dissolved, and the elements shall melt with fervent heat? Nevertheless we, according to his promise, look for new heavens and a new earth, wherein dwelleth righteousness. Wherefore, beloved, seeing that ye look for such things, be diligent that ye may be found of him in peace, without spot, and blameless." 2 Peter 3:9-14

There is no other way to put it; fear God. Do not fear the things of God. For many have deprived themselves of God's love because of the way they deem spiritual things. God's kingdom is coming, the world as we know it shall pass away and there will be a separation between those who have chosen God's ways, and those who decided not to "be religious." Pray for such people to come to peace in Christ.

"And he said unto me, It is done. I am Alpha and Omega, the beginning and the end. I will give unto him that is athirst of the fountain of the water of life freely. He that overcometh shall inherit all things; and I will be his God, and he shall be my son. But the fearful, and unbelieving, and the abominable, and murderers, and whoremongers, and sorcerers, and idolaters, and all liars, shall have their part in the lake which burneth with fire and brimstone: which is the second death." ~ Revelation 21:6-8.

"Thus speaketh the LORD of hosts, saying, This people say, The time is not come, the time that the LORD's house should be built. Then came the word of the LORD by Haggai the prophet, saying, Is it time for you, O ye, to dwell in your ceiled houses, and this house lie waste? Now

therefore thus saith the LORD of hosts; Consider your ways. Ye have sown much, and bring in little; ye eat, but ye have not enough; ye drink, but ye are not filled with drink; ye clothe you, but there is none warm; and he that earneth wages earneth wages to put it into a bag with holes. Thus saith the LORD of hosts; Consider your ways. Go up to the mountain, and bring wood, and build the house; and I will take pleasure in it, and I will be glorified, saith the LORD. Ye looked for much, and, lo it came to little; and when ye brought it home, I did blow upon it. Why? saith the LORD of hosts. Because of mine house that is waste, and ye run every man unto his own house. Therefore the heaven over you is stayed from dew, and the earth is stayed from her fruit." Haggai 1:2-10.

"Now we beseech you, brethren, by the coming of our Lord Jesus Christ, and by our gathering together unto him, That ye be not soon shaken in mind, or be troubled, neither by spirit, nor by word, nor by letter as from us, as that the day of Christ is at hand. Let no man deceive you by any means: for that day shall not come, except there come a falling away first, and that man of sin be revealed, the son of perdition; Who opposeth and exalteth himself above all that is called God, or that is worshipped; so that he as God sitteth in the temple of God, shewing himself that he is God. Remember ye not, that, when I was yet with you, I told you these things? And now ye know what withholdeth that he might be revealed in his time. For the mystery of iniquity doth already work: only he who now letteth will let, until he be taken out of the way. And then shall that Wicked be revealed, whom the Lord shall consume with the spirit of his mouth, and shall destroy with the brightness of his coming: *Even him, whose coming is after the working of Satan with all power and signs and lying wonders, And with all deceivableness of unrighteousness in them that perish; because they received not the love of the truth, that they might be saved. And for this cause God shall send them strong delusion, that they should believe a lie: That they all might be damned who believed not the truth, but had pleasure in unrighteousness."* 2 Thess 2:1-12

You have a choice, to choose the way of righteousness and have everything to gain, nothing to lose. Or you could stay in unbelief, and be possibly damned. Often we hear unbelievers say if God loved the world, then why does he allow us to suffer and cause bad things to happen. Let's see what the bible has to say about that one;

"Thus speaketh the Lord of hosts, saying, Execute true judgment, and show mercy and compassions every man to his brother: And oppress not the widow, nor the fatherless, the stranger, nor the poor; and let none of you imagine evil against his brother in your heart. But they refused to hearken, and pulled away the shoulder, and stopped their ears, that they should not hear. Yea, they made their hearts as an adamant stone, lest they should hear the law, and the words which the Lord of hosts hath sent in his spirit by the former prophets: therefore came a great wrath from the Lord of hosts. Therefore it is come to pass, that as he cried, and they would not hear; so they cried, and I would not hear, saith the Lord of hosts" Zechariah 7:9-13

God is not unjust. This piece of scripture puts it very clearly;

"In the day of prosperity be joyful, but in the day of adversity consider: God also hath set the one over against the other, to the end that man should find nothing after him." Ecclesiastes 7:14

God is not out to make our lives miserable. In Isaiah 57:16 He reveals;

"For I will not contend for ever neither will I be always wroth: for the spirit should fail before me, and the souls which I have made." And again in Lamentations: "For the LORD will not cast off for ever: But though he cause grief, yet will he have compassion according to the multitude of his mercies. For he doth not afflict willingly nor grieve the children of men. To crush under his feet all the prisoners of the earth. To turn aside the right of a man before the face of the most High, To subvert a man in his cause, the LORD approveth not. Who is he that saith, and it cometh to pass, when the Lord commandeth it not? Out of the mouth of the most High proceedeth not evil and good? Wherefore doth a living man complain, a man for the punishment of his sins? Let us search and try our ways, and turn again to the LORD. Let us lift up our heart with our hands unto God in the heavens." Lamentations 3:31-41

"Say to them, 'As surely as I live, declares the Sovereign Lord, I take no pleasure in the death of the wicked, but rather that they turn from their ways and live. Turn! Turn

from your evil ways! Why will you die, O house of Israel?'
Ezekiel 33:11

Yet the children of thy people say, The way of the Lord is not equal: but as for them, their way is not equal."
Ezekiel 33: 17

As my pastor, puts it, when Adam and Eve fell it gave the devil authority to rule over the earth that belongs to God. What the second Adam came to do was to win it back fair game by coming as a man that could be tempted, suffered crucifixion with no bail out from the Supernatural power just so every person willing could claim back son-ship to God alone. In the Old Testament days, before grace, the sinners would be cut off and the few righteous or obedient as it were, would be spared:

"And they shall bear the punishment of their iniquity: the punishment of the prophet shall be even as the punishment of him that seeketh unto him; That the house of Israel may go no more astray from me, neither be polluted any more with all their transgressions; but that they may be my people, and I may be their God, saith the Lord GOD. The word of the LORD came again to me, saying, Son of man, when the land sinneth against me by trespassing grievously, then will I stretch out mine hand upon it, and will break the staff of the bread thereof, and will send famine upon it, and will cut off man and beast from it:[…] Though Noah, Daniel, and Job were in it, as I live, saith the Lord GOD, they shall deliver neither son nor daughter; they shall but deliver their own souls by their

righteousness. For thus saith the Lord GOD; How much more when I send my four sore judgments upon Jerusalem, the sword, and the famine, and the noisome beast, and the pestilence, to cut off from it man and beast? Yet, behold, therein shall be left a remnant that shall be brought forth, both sons and daughters: behold, they shall come forth unto you, and ye shall see their way and their doings: and ye shall be comforted concerning the evil that I have brought upon Jerusalem, even concerning all that I have brought upon it. And they shall comfort you, when ye see their ways and their doings: and ye shall know that I have not done without cause all that I have done in it, saith the Lord GOD." Ezekiel 14:10-23

God does nothing without cause, and as the verse above shows, God will send pestilence if that will grab your attention if nothing else will.

"Behold, the Lord's hand is not shortened, that it cannot save; neither his ear heavy, that it cannot hear: But your iniquities have separated between you and your God, and your sins have hid his face from you, that he will not hear." Isaiah 59:1-2

Thank God for Jesus Christ, because of his obedience we all can be forgiven again and again. However we are still living in a world of deception, when we willingly choose to disregard our Maker whom we belong to; he can still bring judgment. It astounds me how none of us had the power to create ourselves, yet we think we have the power to live our lives anyhow we like. God reminds us in Isaiah 45:9-10:

"Woe unto him that striveth with his Maker! Let the potsherd strive with the potsherds of the earth. Shall the clay say to him that fashioneth it, what makest thou? Or thy work, He hath no hands? Woe unto him that saith unto his father, What begettest thou? or to the woman, What hast thou brought forth?"

God is crying out to you, "A son honoureth his father, and a servant his master: if then I be a father, where is mine honour? And I be a master, where is my fear? Saith the Lord of hosts unto you." Malachi 1:6

"Ye have said, It is vain to serve God: and what profit is it that we have walked mournfully before the Lord of hosts. And now we call the proud happy; yea, they that work wickedness are set up; yea, they that tempt God are even delivered. Then they that feared the LORD spake often one to another: and the LORD hearkened, and heard it, and a book of remembrance was written before him for them that feared the LORD, and that thought upon his name. And they shall be mine, saith the LORD of hosts, in that day when I make up my jewels; and I will spare them, as a man spareth his own son that serveth him. Then shall ye return, and discern between the righteous and the wicked, between him that serveth God and him that serveth him not." Malachi 3:14-18

Do a Google search on how many Christians there are in the world. Then study what these people have in common, what made them make that decision, evaluate the probability of those people being wrong. May you and I be counted among those that have made that choice to be committed to our Maker. Thank God for Jesus, before Him it was covenant law, you sin you die, the wrath of God would fall unless a prophet interceded, but now by grace anyone and everyone can pray to the Father. Don't be afraid to do God's instruction. The word of God says He confirmeth the word of his servant, and performeth the counsel of his messengers. God is searching for complete and devout selflessness where we lay things to heart when His word, his love and his grace are disregarded.

Jeremiah 12:10-11 tells us; *"Many pastors have destroyed my vineyard, they have trodden my portion under foot, they have made my pleasant portion a desolate wilderness. They have made it desolate, and being desolate it mourneth unto me; the whole land is made desolate, because no man layeth it to heart."* While Ezekiel 34:4-6 laments; *"You have not strengthened the weak or healed the sick or bound up the injured. You have not brought back the strays or searched for the lost. [...] So they were scattered because there was no shepherd, and when they were scattered they became food for all the wild animals."*

We can no longer afford to have dry and lukewarm churches, only concerned with programs and survival while disregarding the power we have already been given by Christ. Be mighty for God. *Ephesians 6:10* urges us to *"Be strong in the lord and in the power of his might,"* and the Old Testament is an inspiring place to go to for accounts of diligent men and women of

God. In I Chronicles we encounter the story of David in the caves hiding from Saul. When Saul dies, many mighty men come to fight with David. In chapter 9 verse 13 these men are described as 'very able men for the work of the service of the house of God' and in chapter 11:15-19 we are told how they risked their lives to get their leader water from the well of Bethlehem;

"Now three of the thirty captains went down to the rock to David, into the cave of Adullam; and the host of the Philistines encamped in the valley of Rephaim. And David was then in the hold, and the Philistines' garrison was then at Bethlehem. And David longed, and said, Oh that one would give me drink of the water of the well of Bethlehem, that is at the gate! And the three brake through the host of the Philistines, and drew water out of the well of Bethlehem, that was by the gate, and took it, and brought it to David: but David would not drink of it, but poured it out to the LORD. And said, My God forbid it me, that I should do this thing: shall I drink the blood of these men that have put their lives in jeopardy? for with the jeopardy of their lives they brought it. Therefore he would not drink it. These things did these three mightiest."

In 2 Kings 22 we are told of the story of Josiah, one of King Hezekiah's great grandsons. Josiah is an intriguing character, his father Amon came from an evil father Mannaseh, and he fathered Jehoahaz the evil. In between all that evil came forth Josiah tearing down the strongholds and declaring ground for the Lord Almighty. It doesn't matter what environment you are in, or what popular culture around you dictates; it doesn't matter if prayer time and regarding God is not part of your family, on your own you have the power to be mighty for God. May the Lord raise up Josiahs in our generation and send them out as arrows into the field of the earth. The spirit of God today cries out, *"Sow to yourselves in righteousness, reap in mercy; break up your fallow ground: for it is time to seek the LORD, till he come and rain righteousness upon you." Hosea 10:12*

God is searching for men and women who can go down to the deep on their knees and in their hearts. Make up your mind you, to fight for your God. It is a new wave coming, and all men will come to return to their maker, be among the forerunners. Start by praying for your body, your family, your city and soon power will begin to rise in you. We are talking about God's power by the way, not the new age 'believe in yourself, you have the power to achieve anything' mambo-jumbo prevalent in reality television.

"I exhort therefore, that, first of all, supplications, prayers, intercessions, and giving of thanks, be made for all men; For kings, and for all that are in authority; that we may lead a quiet and peaceable life in all godliness and honesty. For this is good and acceptable in the sight of God our Saviour; Who will have all men to be saved, and to come unto the knowledge of the truth. For there is one God, and one mediator between God and men, the man Christ Jesus;

Who gave himself a ransom for all, to be testified in due time." I Timothy 2:1-6

"That the generation to come might know them [the Lord's commandments] even the children which should be born; who should arise and declare them to their children: That they might set their hope in God, and not forget the works of God, but keep his commandments." Psalm 78:6-7

If you are a young adult, the world is looking at you as the next generation, what kind of role model are you for the generations to come. Can people depend on you for wisdom, for values and for kindness? If you are for God, let it show;

"Let no man despise thy youth but be thou an example of the believers in word, in conversation, in charity, in spirit, in purity." I Timothy 4:12

"Wherefore the rather, brethren, give diligence to make your calling and election sure: for if ye do these things (2 Peter 1:4-9) ye shall never fall: For so an entrance shall be ministered unto you abundantly into the everlasting kingdom of our Lord and Saviour Jesus Christ." 2 Peter 1:10

The scripture above suggests that we ensure that we can be identified as Christians. Not hypocritically or self-righteously. I see it as this, sometimes I think of fasting but never get the push to actually do it, but when I call my sister or my best friend and tell them, "I'm going to be fasting for you on Wednesday" I am going to do it to be true to my word. I once pledged to donate some money to a certain organization in January. When January came so many other things had come up as well that needed money, but because I had openly spoken my commitment, I wanted to follow through to uphold my repute as faithful. We are like that as humans, we feel great about ourselves when people feel they can trust us. What Peter was saying in the verse above is if you make it a pattern and a commitment to establish your faith, you will feel more inclined to behave in a manner consistent with what you profess. When you confess that you belong to Jesus, he will indeed say, 'This child is mine' when the devil tries to mess with you. Moreso on the day of judgement he will accept you into the Kingdom of them that remained faithful to Him. Season your speech, while you're being polite don't falter your beliefs, your faith and your aspirations, if you really want something let it show. Yes, there will be a price to pay my dear generation. That price may be a job offer, neglected because your resume shows involvement with a Christian ministry, it could be a relationship, or family that is yet to come to Christ calling you self-righteous, co-workers may avoid you and talk to you differently. The price may be sacrificing certain pleasures you've grown up with, or it may be spiritual attacks as the devil tries to make you quit Christianity and forsake God. He did it to Job, he did it to Jesus; guess what Job got, everything he'd lost doubled, and Jesus got a seat by the right hand side of God and Kingship over God's kingdom. Do not lose hope- it really is better on the Kingdom side. Here is some scripture to encourage you:

"Yet if any man suffer as a Christian, let him not be ashamed, but let him glorify God on this behalf." I Peter 4:16

"Wherefore let them that suffer according to the will of God commit the keeping of their souls to him in well doing, as unto a faithful Creator." I Peter 4:18

"But ye are a chosen generation, a royal priesthood, an holy nation, a peculiar people; that ye should show forth the praises of him who hath called you out of darkness into his marvellous light." 2:9

"Give thanks unto the Lord, call upon his name, make known his deeds among the people." I Chronicles 16:8-12

"Anyone who joins himself to the Lord is accepted." Isaiah 56:3-7

Give God all the glory, oh how He loves you and is well pleased with you!

*

"Seeing ye have purified your souls in obeying the truth through the Spirit unto unfeigned love of the brethren, see that ye love one another with a pure heart fervently." I Peter 1:22

Now I want to talk about love. If you're like me, the commandment to love one another is one that I feel is the easiest to follow and doesn't sound too demanding, it's covered, I smile and not think too spiritually about it. But what does it really mean to love someone fervently and with a pure heart. Take a look at this:

"My brethren, have not the faith of our Lord Jesus Christ, the Lord of glory, with respect of persons. For if there come unto your assembly a man with a gold ring, in goodly apparel, and there come in also a poor man in vile raiment; And ye have respect to him that weareth the gay clothing, and say unto him, Sit thou here in a good place; and say to the poor, Stand thou there, or sit here under my footstool: Are ye not then partial in yourselves, and are become judges of evil thoughts? Hearken, my beloved brethren, Hath not God chosen the poor of this world rich in faith, and heirs of the kingdom which he hath promised to them that love him? But ye have despised the poor. Do not rich men oppress you, and draw you before the judgment seats? Do not they blaspheme that worthy name by the which ye are called? If ye fulfil the royal law according to the scripture, Thou shalt love thy neighbour as thyself, ye do well: But if ye have respect to persons, ye commit sin, and are convinced of the law as transgressors. For whosoever shall keep the whole law, and yet offend in one point, he is guilty of all." James 2:1-10

Say someone well dressed walks into church, we tend to treat them with honour and perhaps even feel they are better than us. But if someone is dressed off and talks unlearnedly, we easily treat them poorly. We need to love and honour each other, yes even the ones that rub us off the wrong way. We would have to eventually see over faults and vices and just love. What value do we place on someone else? Isn't it startling how we meet someone, maybe speak with them for a few minutes and immediately determine what they seem to be able to offer. Any person at any given time has not lived out everything they can, therefore it is unduly to approximate their value by our view of their lives.

"Judge not according to the appearance, but judge righteous judgment." John 7:24

I have been blessed and privileged to meet and be ministered to by Pastor Paul Lee, a dedicated man of God from South Korea in his seventies. I love him dearly and it is evident to see God's love upon his life. I want to share what he said during a bible study meeting; that fellowship was on the basis of being children of God, not on our personalities, flaws and faults- so we shouldn't focus on these. What is your capacity to love? Are you willing to love only what you are enculturated to, what you prefer and what you want or do you have Christ's capacity to love unconditionally? The un-loveable, those people we can't stand but God still uses them, shows them visions, answers their prayers and blesses and we think, God really? Then we start to think, why are they being blessed- why does their stuff work out when they don't even really do what

God wants them to do- hey here's a tip, let Him do it, at least he'll cover that part of bless your enemies on our behalf. In all situations, you need to maintain your capacity to love. Perhaps you have asked yourself, Why do the ones who hurt us and leave us when we've been so good to them end up looking happier than us and getting what they want before us? I never could quite answer that question myself, logically, good things go to good people and bad things go to bad people and God is ours so that He can answer our prayers right, doesn't he invite us to taste Him? Doesn't He tell us He wants to give us the desires of our hearts and yes, lift the needy from the ash-heap and sit them among princes? But one thing I've learnt is God's ways are always going to be higher than ours. But then again, you think, we do the right things, we don't conform to the world and we try to do what God says we should do and when we fall short we are truly repentant and ask for forgiveness and try not to do the same things, doesn't God see that? Then I learnt God does things for HIS righteousness' sake, not ours; lest we become arrogant or fail to enjoy the life he has given us trying to be righteous. When we bank on our own ability to do the right thing, we tend to lose sight of God's hand of grace when we do the right thing. God also wants to know that we love Him just because He is God, and not because of what He can do for us. In all, remember that God's ways are always going to be higher than ours. Above all, love your God;

"Hear therefore, O Israel, and observe to do it; that it may be well with thee, and that ye may increase mightily, as the Lord God of thy fathers hath promised thee, in the land that floweth with milk and honey. Hear O, Israel: The Lord our God is one Lord: And thou shalt love the Lord thy God with all thine heart, and with all thy soul, and with all thy might[…] And thou shalt teach them diligently unto thy children, and shalt talk of them when thou sittest in thine house, and when thou walkest by the way, and when thou liest down, and when thou risest up." Deut 6 vs 3-7

May our generation love God so much, the angels should be praising God in a new way because of it. May God be able to say, Hear therefore, O World, and not just Israel, as the whole world begins to lift up His name. I do want to see such glory in my lifetime; people from different cultures, young and old; getting together in their numbers for all nighters' conferences and concerts where God's name is praised. May disciples of Jesus be birthed across nations. May we achieve fellowship, and may we achieve ministries.

You may be thinking that you are not called or gifted to do ministry; I would like to tell you not to underestimate how we impact the kingdom of God when we give into a ministry, be it monetarily, in prayer or giving of our time and abilities. If you are like me, we observe with a critical eye when televangelists are promoting their material. I want to feel that the minister is not glorifying themselves, and that the precious word of God is not turned into a commodity. I learnt to be wise, yet simple minded about sowing into a ministry uniquely. There have been times in my life when I had moved to a new city and longing for a place of worship or to meet with other believers I could relate with, or just go to a church where the worship was reviving and encouraging, and found none. Such were the times when online sermons and worship songs on youtube nourished me. Most churches are struggling to be on air. Many others have suffered from the double-edged sword of fighting for survival while also trying to reach souls. I have come to a matured understanding of how advancing the kingdom of God is advancing his ministries too. After our judgements and scrutiny of televangelists, we have to use discernment and wisdom to be able to see that we are not "advancing" a person, but we are deliberately advancing everything Jesus. After we have prayed for men and women of God not to fall, but overcome, we should try to help them broadcast a message that may touch a suicidal father, an out-casted son or teach a habit changing revelation or sow a seed that will touch those in need in far places we can't reach ourselves. What it all says is simply, 'God I care about what you plan to do in the end.'

Whatever the case, we need to ask God for wisdom on how to live in this free market and unstable economy. Be diligent, the word of God says if a man loves to sleep he shall not eat. Whatever you get a chance to do, do it well and you will have increase. Practice moderation and foresight, save your assets if you cannot yet save money, protect your health by watching what you put in your mouth; it may save you thousands of dollars when you are retired. You have the power to feel good about your financial decisions. While you are at it, don't forget to give. I heard someone once say how you spend your money is a reflection of what's important to you. Is advancing God's kingdom important to you? How much…

Today start by praying for your nation. Psalm 144:12-15 gives us a template;

"That our sons may be as plants grown up in their youth; that our daughters may be as corner stones, polished after the similitude of a palace: That our garners may be full, affording all manner of store: that our sheep may bring forth thousands and ten thousands in our streets: That our oxen may be strong to labour; that there be no breaking in, nor going out; that there be no complaining in our streets. Happy is that people, that is in such a case: yea, happy is that people, whose God is the Lord."

Then pray for nations far away, for the glory of God to fall on them like how it falls in a powerful service, Psalm 63 verses 1-2 show us how, *"O God, thou art my God; early will I seek thee: my soul thirsteth for thee, my flesh longeth for thee in a dry and thirsty land, where no water is; To see thy power and thy glory, so as I have seen thee in the sanctuary."*

Lord, may we now begin to see your power out-

side the church, and in the world.

God is longing to restore man back to himself as it was with Adam, but he had to create a brand new incorruptible kingdom, and he did through Christ. The seed that was indeed tempted by the enemy, but incorruptible to the death, he overcame just to bring mankind back to God and that's all God is saying! It is up to us to grow the kingdom of heaven. Long for it for your family, your former school mates, your neighbourhood and your home town. Long for all your kith and kin to make it to this glorious place of rest, of no death and no pain.

I read Revelation chapter 21 one day and just began weeping. It was so real to me I started calling out names even of people I didn't quite like yet and saying they will attain salvation. May God give us clean commitments to praying for others and being there for them; and clean commitments to God himself.

"Finally, be ye all of one mind, having compassion one of another, love as brethren, be pitiful, be courteous: Not rendering evil for evil, or railing for railing: but contrariwise blessing; knowing that ye are thereunto called, that ye should inherit a blessing. For he that will love life, and see good days, let him refrain his tongue from evil, and his lips that they speak no guile: Let him eschew evil, and do good; let him seek peace, and ensue it. For the eyes of the Lord are over the righteous, and his ears are open unto their prayers: but the face of the Lord is against them that do

evil. And who is he that will harm you, if ye be followers of that which is good? But and if ye suffer for righteousness' sake, happy are ye: and be not afraid of their terror, neither be troubled; But sanctify the Lord God in your hearts: and be ready always to give an answer to every man that asketh you a reason of the hope that is in you with meekness and fear: Having a good conscience; that, whereas they speak evil of you, as of evildoers, they may be ashamed that falsely accuse your good conversation in Christ." 1 Peter 3:8-16

"For as the earth bringeth forth her bud, and as the garden causeth the things that are sown in it to spring forth; so the Lord God will cause righteousness thereof go forth as brightness, and the salvation thereof as a lamp that burneth." Isaiah 61:11- 62:1

"Also the sons of the stranger, that join themselves to the Lord, to serve him, and to love the name of the Lord, to be his servants every one that keepeth the Sabbath from polluting it, and taketh hold of my covenant; Even them will I bring to my holy mountain, and make them joyful in my house of prayer: their burnt offerings and their sacrifices shall be accepted upon mine altar; for mine house shall be called an house of prayer for all people." Isaiah 56:6-7

Isaiah 51:7-8 "Hearken unto me, ye that know righteousness, the people in whose heart is my law; fear ye not the reproach of men, neither be ye afraid of their revilings. For the moth shall eat them up like a garment, and the worm shall eat them like wool: but my righteousness shall be for ever, and my salvation from generation to generation." Isaiah 51: 7-8

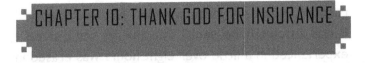

CHAPTER 10: THANK GOD FOR INSURANCE

"The angel of the Lord encamps around those who
fear him, and he delivers them" Psalm 34:7

*

I never associate having to pre-pay for a mishap with
anything good. One boxing-day morning I thanked
God for those greedy companies that make tonnes
of money from our dearly beloved pay checks each
month. A cousin of mine and I had rented a car and
driven around three cities through wet snow and rain
on boxing day, for the love of shopping. It wasn't until
the time came to return the rental did the tires slip
and ram into a tree... in my driveway! The right tail
light was broken and the rear of that silver Ford focus
was outrageously dented. The repairs would have cost
me over a thousand dollars, an accident report that
would have tainted my driving record and increased
my premium. My sleep was restless and the snooze
button did not mean a thing to me the next morning.
I called the rental company, a lovely lady picked up
the phone, probably her first call for the day; my fears
and dread were expressed and the response I got
back came like the first day of summer, "No, you're
good, you had insurance." I could not believe it, and so
after I put the phone down I called her back again and
asked, 'Well will this little accident go on my driver's

record?" Again her sweet words, "No, you're good." It was absolutely heavenly! The anxiety and distress I experienced in a little over eight hours was erased in a matter of seconds. All I could say was thank God for car insurance!

The blood of Jesus gives us such a guarantee and more. Because Christ was crucified on Calvary, we are rest assured upon receiving and confessing Him as our Lord and Saviour, we have hope for a life of peace and comfort in knowing we are not on our own. Because of the blood of Jesus we have the right and the power to turn destruction and distress into righteousness, peace and joy. Because of the mighty blood of Christ, we have the right to speak to anything the devil throws at us and command it to flee in His name. We have an assurance that our lives do have a purpose and that God who created mankind will receive us back to eternal glory. We cannot be condemned forever, we may sin and fall short, our families, friends, finances and occupations may seem to spit us out or disapprove of our choices, but because Christ will not condemn us, we have assurance.

If you were to ask me how I know I've done the right thing to surrender to Christ, I would tell you because I have found a certain joy that always and for sure comes after dealing with heart-breaking and difficult situations in my life. Sometimes I get beat down, discouraged and tired, then after crying some or feeling sorry for myself, an inexplicable joy comes upon me when I bring my mind back to saying that God is good and through Christ, He will hear me when I call. What a blessed assurance. We have this insurance that no matter what and after all has been said and done, all we have to do is surrender ourselves to Christ; present our situations to him, and it is FINISHED- by the blood of the Lamb.

So dear beloved, for any situation that is to confront you, for every place you find yourself in, open your mouth and say, 'Whatever the case, whatever the outcome, I trust God. Whatever happens or does not happen; God has it under control.' In fact for every trying time of your life, tame yourself to say, 'If anything, I want this period of my life to go down as the time I trusted God with my all. I want the angels to be saying God this child trusts you!'

Remember also, that whatever you failed at in the past, whatever you did or didn't do, you are also redeemed from that. Say this prayer one day, 'Father let not my past, even my most recent past, be a hindrance to moving forward.' It doesn't matter where you've come from, what you've done, or what you may have told people or attested to, move forward in freedom. You are not condemned in Christ. We need to learn to tap into that grace though, by working in His will using His word and Spirit as our guide.

Proverbs 16:2-3; 7 "All the ways of a man are clean in his own eyes; but the LORD weigheth the spirits. Commit thy works unto the LORD, and thy thoughts shall be established. [...] When a man's ways please the LORD, he maketh even his enemies to be at peace with him."

God loves us unconditionally, but we are responsible over whether He is pleased with us. We have a blessed assurance, but we need to endeavour to walk in a manner that is pleasing to our Father. As the verse above reveals, when we please God, everything around us comes to a point of peace. Let's see what the bible says is the best way to please God.

In Matthew 22:36-40 A Pharisee lawyer asks Christ, *'Master which is the great commandment in the law?' Jesus said unto him,*

'Thou shalt love the Lord thy God with all thy heart, and with all thy soul, and with all thy mind. This is the first and great commandment. And the second is like unto it; Thou shalt love thy neighbour as thyself. On these two commandments hang all the law and the prophets.'

Love is key to understanding the heart of God. All you need to do is fall in love with God. I am in love with my husband. I remember every step of falling in love with him and how everyday I think about him and want to be with him only. We all have had that feeling. When you love someone, you want to do anything for them and make them happy and it is so easy to want to show love to them. I get excited when I am doing something to show love to my husband. Much in the same way, God wants you to fall in love with Him. When you fall in love with God, you want to stop arguing with Him, you want to make him happy, you want to do things for Him and you want the whole world to see your love. In the verse above we are told by Christ himself that the greatest commandment is to love your God with all your heart, your soul and mind. Do your emotions and beliefs reflect ultimate love for God? What is near and dear to you in your heart? Is it the Lord your God? Think about it. When you have begun to really love God, your erstwhile beliefs mean nothing anymore and you are not nostalgic about a life with no yardstick. You are prepared to do anything that God would rather have you do.

After loving God, Christ informs us that the next best thing to do is to love people the same way you love yourself. Now honestly speaking, is it not way easier to love an invisible God who as such could never rub you the wrong way, or literally say anything to you to hurt your feelings, than loving everyone the same way as we love ourselves! Of course we know that a whole part of loving God means loving the people he created.

I have shared how I have been tremendously blessed by various men and women of God at various points in my lifetime. It is a good thing to belong to a church family, and be devout members and serve where you are planted. But I count myself truly blessed for all the displacement that has taken place in my life. God has taken me to many places in my youth, where I have had the chance to sit under different ministers and be blessed by their various gifts. One of the women I am blessed to have met is Pastor Pat Francis. In one sermon, she said these words very simply and gently, and for the first time in my life, I understood what kindness meant. She said, be kind at home. I realized how I had mood swings towards my siblings, my room-mates or my aunt I lived with for some time. I know this is prevalent in many homes, we do not often show kindness to one another in our own houses. We yell at our children, we feel disgraced by our parents and we do not openly encourage our siblings. What is it? We are to love others as we love ourselves. Learn to believe in other's people's intentions, people may hurt you but didn't really mean to, or may be truly repentant after they do. Let's spread the net, charity begins at home, after learning to love those in your own household, learn to love your co-workers, mates, neighbours and those people you see constantly. Christ did not say scrutinize them sharply to hate their flaws, He said love them the same way you love yourself! That's gotta hurt!

Throughout this book I have endeavoured to explain Christianity or Spirituality, biblically. I do not know how this can be described biblically but it is a phenomenon I have witnessed on several occasions. In my mother tongue we call it, 'kushurwa,' and as un-Christian as it may sound, it can be familiarized with being jinxed! I'll give you an example; a church was planning an event and there was poor communication amongst the planners and disgruntlement amongst the individuals delegated with various tasks for the event. This in turn caused the members of the church to recall other faults of the leader and it soon became a huge deal that the members were reluctant to pray and cover their leader. When the time for the event came, the leader suffered so many attacks including robbery, loss of property; the event itself, although had been long prayed over and anticipated, turned out poorly. A certain unintentional satisfaction that seemed to say, 'I told you so,' was among the members. Of course deep down inside they did not mean their leader any harm, they love their leader, however the thoughts and hurt they harboured against the leader's faults, were used by the enemy as a tool to inhibit intercession and a sacrifice of joy while serving God. In another situation, a pastor's wife had a brawl with one of the ladies in the church. She became so bitter and hurt inside and unknowingly wanted vengeance. The lady involved fell ill and lost her job and the pastor's wife made mention that this lady fell ill just after fighting with her. Christian listen closely, the enemy uses principalities and powers that you cannot be ignorant of, do not curse another child of God just so your point can be proved. Let God avenge you in his way, Christ commanded us to give the other cheek when we are bruised, to never ask if someone borrows and does not return. Do not let your wounded pride or even rightful feelings cause the downfall of another. When you see another man fall, how can you rejoice at his downfall? We have one enemy and that is Satan only. Remember that especially in times when you are hurt, it is part of the Christian test.

Let's move on, the next cohort that we need to love on is the sinner. The soul that is living in sin, and does what we hate and shun. Can you imagine Christ also wants us to love these individuals the *same* way we love ourselves! Think about that more deeply. We mostly hate our governments, we hate murderers, rapists, atheists and mockers; and God is saying to love them? Like ourselves? There's another mystery right there. Only grace can enable us to do the impossible. It also takes a broken heart to truly understand Christ's love for the sinner. We are keeping in mind that the sin is to be hated. This is the story of grace, we tend to think we are better off and doing good because we made the right choices and we are better, but fail to realize that we have merely been given grace. Only when you fall do you realize that you truly are weak on your own. For some people, they quickly and easily master meekness and recognize God's grace; these people are usually the soft-hearted and gentle people. For some of us, it took making mistakes and falling into sin to realize that on our own we are truly weak. When you realize this, you can understand how others too can be weak. Christ had compassion for the sinner, who are we to think we have the right to judge and condemn the sinner? Do not ever be blinded about hating the sinner and not the sin. We have one enemy who is the devil. Love the sinners and pray for them as you would pray for yourself. People living without a care of God's word are living in affliction. They are tormented by the enemy so much such that they have become callous to God's being. They have adopted ways "not to care" but deep inside, all mankind longs for God's presence of powerful peace and protection over them.

Other people may still love the Lord deep inside, but something has dampened their faith and they have lost touch of the things of God, and they just need particular middleware. Middleware is software that connects the low level operating system to high level applications. The world is full of stagnant believers who have somehow or suddenly lost their functionality, and are simply missing that one word, or atmosphere that will help them operate again at a high level of faith. Christians, we cannot afford not to love the lost. Certainly there will be some battles we cannot fight and we have to be careful to guard our own faith when dealing with people whose hearts are cold towards God. The bible warns us in Romans 16 verse 17-18; *"Now I beseech you, brethren, mark them which cause divisions and offences contrary to the doctrine which ye have learned; and avoid them, For they that are such serve not our Lord Jesus Christ, but their own belly; and by good words and fair speeches deceive the hearts of the simple.*" Some people will only just argue and want to downplay your faith, it is not every moment we are to accommodate such attitudes as a gesture of love. God has given us both the wisdom to persuade others of the good news of the gospel; and the authority to shake the dust off our feet and walk away. It is through the Holy Spirit that we will know when to apply either. We must keep moving knowing we have the blood of Jesus backing us up no matter what.

"Little children, it is the last time: and as ye have heard that antichrist shall come even now are there many antichrists; whereby we know that it is the last time [...] But ye have an unction from the Holy One, and ye know all things." I John 2:18; 20

God will also be faithful to remind us when we begin to take his word the wrong way. Look at the story of Jonah for an example. When Jonah had hesitated going to Ninevah to proclaim judgement, God sabotaged his disobedience and Jonah found himself uttering God's judgement. Now the people repented so God spared them. You can imagine what Jonah was thinking these people thought of him, the prophet of doom who wanted them dead- or just plainly the false prophet, so he got really upset that God had not carried out the word of destruction he had given him to speak. But God reminds him it was not about him, but about fulfilling God's will. So imagine how in all things God is with us.

Now if you are in Christ and struggling with sin yourself, or are feeling overwhelmed with 'God's rules' remember Christians are not super humans. We are human living in a world of sin and darkness, emptiness and sabotage. We get afflicted too the minute we step outside of God's presence. I am writing to tell you today, when affliction comes in like a flood, raise up a loud cry unto God saying, "Father, cause me now to kill tens of thousands like David." God will surely strengthen you to fight every thought and feeling and situation that comes from the enemy. Child of God, be strong in the Lord. If you would command that nothing happens in your life that God doesn't want and believe that prayer with absolutely no doubt, knowing that all you need is His grace, not your intelligence, your sound mind, your assets, your goodness- just His grace, that grace shall be sufficient for all your needs. You need God's presence in your life and it is your mission each day to maintain that Godly atmosphere. It is crucial to fortify your life as a city. This entails keeping your activities under the parameters of God's word, and keeping your words deliberately in line with God's spirit in you. God will surely bless you, and when He starts to bless you, receive His blessings graciously. When God wants to do something for you, nothing can stop Him, and He can use anything to show you his goodness. Be on the lookout for God showing you favour and kindness. Recognize what things in your life happened because of God's grace coming upon you. There were times when people have come into my life and blessed me magnanimously even when I had not done anything for them, nor had shown them particular affinity. It is unbelievable how many strangers have gone out of their way for me. People I'd never really helped in their time of need have come to meet my needs. Each time this has happened I have always felt such a burden to want to repay their kindness just to show my deep gratitude. I have not yet found those opportunities monetarily to bless these people. It took me quite a while to recognize that yes even through people, God was showing me his loving-kindness, and I could never repay God with anything else but to love Him and testify of His love. I also learnt a big lesson that only God rewards, therefore our part is to learn to earnestly speak blessing over those God has used to bless you. This way, you realize that it is not you who blesses, but God. You remain meek and realize that you can learn to earnestly pray for people you otherwise wouldn't care less about.

We are attracted to Godliness because it guarantees the fullness of life;

"Thou wilt show me the path of life: in thy presence is fullness of joy; at thy right hand there are pleasures for evermore." Psalm 16:11

"Trust in the Lord, and do good; so shalt thou dwell in the land, and verily thou shalt be fed. Delight thyself also in the Lord: and he shall give thee the desires of thine heart. Commit thy way unto the Lord; trust also in him; and he shall

bring it to pass. And he shall bring forth thy righteousness as the light, and thy judgment as the noonday. Rest in the Lord, and wait patiently for him: fret not thyself because of him who prospereth in his way, because of the man who bringeth wicked devices to pass. Cease from anger, and forsake wrath: fret not thyself in any wise to do evil. For evildoers shall be cut off: but those that wait upon the Lord, they shall inherit the earth." Psalm 37:3-9

"Beloved, believe not every spirit, but try the spirits whether they are of God: because many false prophets are gone out into the world. Hereby know ye the Spirit of God: Every spirit that confesseth that Jesus Christ is come in the flesh is of God: And every spirit that confesseth not that Jesus Christ is come in the flesh is not of God: and this is that spirit of antichrist, whereof ye have heard that it should come; and even now already is it in the world. Ye are of God, little children, and have overcome them: because greater is he that is in you, than he that is in the world. They are of the world: therefore speak they of the world, and the world heareth them. We are of God: he that knoweth God heareth us; he that is not of God heareth not us. Hereby know we the spirit of truth, and the spirit of error." I John 4: 1-6

"Beloved if our heart condemn us not, then have we confidence toward God. And whatsoever we ask, we receive of him, because we keep his commandments, and do those things that are pleasing in his sight. And this is his commandment, That we should believe on the name of his Son Jesus Christ, and love one another, as he gave us commandment. And he that keepeth his commandments dwelleth in him, and he in him. And hereby we know that

he abideth in us, by the Spirit which he hath given us." I
John 3: 21-24

Again, I want to say, do not fear the things of God, but
rather love God.

"And we have known and believed the love that
God hath to us. God is love; and he that dwelleth in love
dwelleth in God, and God in him. Herein is our love made
perfect, that we may have boldness in the day of judgment:
because as he is, so are we in this world. There is no fear
in love; but perfect love casteth out fear: because fear hath
torment. He that feareth is not made perfect in love." I
John 4: 16-18

If you really want God, you'll find him;

"With the merciful thou wilt show thyself merciful;
with an upright man thou wilt show thyself upright; with
the pure thou wilt show thyself pure; and with the forward
thou wilt show thyself forward." ~ Psalm 18:25-26

John 12:46-50: "I am come a light into the world, that
whosoever believeth on me should not abide in darkness.
And if any man hear my words, and believe not, I judge
him not: for I came not to judge the world, but to save
the world. He that rejecteth me, and receiveth not my
words, hath one that judgeth him: the word that I have
spoken, the same shall judge him in the last day. For I have
not spoken of myself; but the Father which sent me, he
gave me a commandment, what I should say, and what
I should speak. And I know that his commandment is life

everlasting: whatsoever I speak therefore, even as the Father said unto me, so I speak."

When God looks at us, he sees his own creation. What God wants from us is to see and live like we know that we are returning back to him. Let this faith in God that you have been freely given not become stultifying in practice, for there is a God territory we are headed to and everything is good in that place; there is acceptance, love, peace, health, no sorrow, no toil and no inequality. Hallelujah.

CHAPTER 11: FROM MY HEART

I don't know the names of many flowers, nor the seasons they grow in, but I like them. I like unique stones. I could go for a walk in the middle of nowhere to search for them, and find somewhere to put them. I love potatoes with no skin and I like doing weird dances when no one is watching...in fact I do it all the time. On beat up days, I like to dress up and walk in expensive shops looking like I could afford buying a ridiculously priced item...*only it didn't come in the right colour.*

I have also endured many struggles in my lifetime. I have struggled with finding where and how to fit in, figuring out what I have been gifted to do and how to do it. My countenance seems to always be down even when I am not particularly sad. I secretly await my heyday and to see the faces of every person who has ever looked down on me...*I am not yet a saint.*

If you were my friend, this is what I would wish for you...

May God arise and begin to take away every uncertainty, every unknown and every grim place in your life right now.

"For thou wilt light my candle: the Lord God will enlighten my darkness. For by thee I have run through a troop, and by my God have I leaped over a wall." ~ Psalm 18:28-29.

May God teach you how to fight, and how to win...

"He teacheth my hands to war, so that a bow of steel is broken by mine arms." ~ Psalm 18:34.

When things start happening, may God shield you and cover you from people that may pull you down, and may God shield you from the pride of man...you know, those people who think you would have never made it had it not been for them...and forget that all of our help comes from the Lord.

"Thou shalt hide them in the secret of thy presence from the pride of man: thou shalt keep them secretly in a pavilion from the strife of tongues." ~ Psalm 31:20.

May God help you know when to refrain from being quick to agree to the things society utters, but to apply your speech seasoned, knowing when to speak and when to reserve your comments. Not to murmur, and not to destroy with your tongue.

"For the word of God is quick, and powerful, and sharper than any twoedged sword, piercing even to the dividing asunder of soul and spirit, and of the joints and marrow, and is a discerner of the thoughts and intents of the heart." ~ Hebrews 4:12

If you are ever surrounded by negative people trying to disperse their faithless convictions, just bring in God! It's amazing how the following statements silence such, "It's in God's hands" or "My God will supply all my needs."

"Now the God of hope fill you with all joy and peace in believing, that ye may abound in hope, through the power of the Holy Ghost." ~ Romans 5:13

May your hope continue to grow, and may you be filled with joy and peace while you wait patiently for your desires.

"Blessed be the Lord: for he hath shown me his marvellous kindness in a strong city." ~ Psalm 31:21.

Believe in the impossible! What is your 'strong city?' Don't you ever forget that your God is above all; the world systems, people, our bodies, our spirits and all that we have and hope to have. The challenge though, is to have faith that He really is stronger. Faith in God is seen by what we believe in our hearts and what we speak with our mouths. May your every word establish what you want to see God do for you, according to His will. You and I are going to show God that we know how to trust Him, deal?

And so we shall get to work, for the marvellous Kingdom of God...

We would do well to start with each other, as Christians. There are so many Christians who are out there alone. Temptations come and they fall because they have been running on empty for so long. While there are many churches, many books, many broadcasts and many uplifting albums, the body of Christ can be alone and without nourishment. Are churches doing enough outside the regular program, spending time with the unordinary "leaders," or "regulars," are we checking up on each other, our friends, family, are they doing okay spiritually, do they need some spiritual boost and an encouraging environment for their spiritual lives? While advancing the kingdom is about reaching out to the lost, aching for lost cities, pleading for the youth and praying fervently against demonic strongholds-the kingdom of God is also about nourishment of the believer. There will be backsliding, there will be giving up, listlessness, slothfulness and discouragement among us. We need to pay attention to each other, and be there for each other. We build churches but we don't build movements, such that for some a change in location or a limitation in mobility might mean spiritual dryness. The dryness I refer to is something you and I are all too familiar with; being unable to pray, or fast, or feeling the same when we come out of a service. It is also sitting in church with passive looks that tell the preacher so blatantly how his message is not really going anywhere. While we judge how good or bad our pastors are, we are seldom responsive to their messages, we are not encouraging them to keep going deeper by our passivity, dead looks that shout, 'I'm just here because I guess it's good to go to church on Sunday.' We need to ask: What do you want us to do God, about the lack of meat in your sanctuaries?

Have you prayed for everything? You haven't started praying for the Spirit of the living God to move upon that small town. Are you serving in ministry at your church? God needs more service from you by reaching out to that individual who doesn't serve, who you don't know much about, who seems unapproachable, who you have never spoken to. Do you have a brother, a sister, a grandmother, call them and pray with them, ask them to fast for you and it will inspire them to revive their spirits. Are you longing for a just-you day at home, resting, a movie and no visitors? Take a minute before it ends where you pray for someone, whoever comes to your mind. Set aside time for God and time for the things of God. Pick three people you know who are not saved and set aside time each day where you are committed to praying for their salvation, and believe those prayers! Pray for your enemies. When you pray for those that may have hurt you or those people whose actions and characters you just don't get, ask God for them to reap where they have not sown, for God to give them a garment of praise for the spirit of heaviness, for God to replace their spiritually destructive ways with hearts that can learn to fear God.

Ask God to strengthen you again and again, to prepare you again and again. There were numerous times in life when I'd get so angry at myself for not being diligent enough, for not getting to the things I needed to get done, for falling in certain areas and was beginning to feel conscious about how I kept asking God for forgiveness, and that also was frustrating me! I tried so hard to do the right thing by myself until I realized that I can't overcome my weaknesses by myself, I need the spirit of God, to pray more and fast more as I've been yearning. There is a song by Josh Wilson, with the words, 'Saviour Please, keep saving me.' When I listened to the full words of the song, I realized that even if I have been in mighty places with God; uttered bold and fiery prayers and attested to strong discipline in my faith, I am still very vulnerable to falling. I realized how weak I actually am, depending on my own understanding and strength was not going to keep my score perfect in the things of God. I needed God to keep saving me. There were certain things I thought I'd never give in to, and I have, certain things I do not condone and I have found myself smiling powerlessly to those things. It hurts very deeply when you realize you have failed to obey. All the many preachers who have made it to the headlines, or have been talked about through and through in their communities for that one mistake they made, are people who need our love and encouragement. We have to realize that upon this earth we are only striving to perfection, so we are going to fail in some things. When you do fall, realize that God's hand is right there to pick you up and He wants to give you the strength and wisdom to pass the test next time. I am now in love with grace since this realization; it is not about our own righteousness, but God's righteousness. This means that grace is what God gives to us; grace to overcome, grace to have patience, grace to for-bear and grace to be saved. So grace you see, is an amazing gift that I have come to realize, we should always be asking more of!

We have failed at many things in life, but even with broken limbs we will get there...

God's mercy is not like man's, it comes with no condition and it is not deliberated. If you are hurting, and are tired of this world, tell Jesus, 'Lord I've been talking to people and they can't talk back to my life, now I want to just talk to you. Spirit of God teach me how to ask for my heart's desires for the word says whatsoever you shall ask in my name, you will receive.' (Mark 11 verses 22-24)

Be encouraged, you are going to be alright. The race however, is still on- so after uplifting words, you need words of empowerment. Do not ever be fooled, you are not a Christian just so you can feel safe and happy inside. You were made a Christian so that you too can have the power to bring back to God what the devil has stolen. You are a child of God so that you know how to access the power to come back to righteousness, the power to perceive, plan and pursue. You have the power to be a God fearing you at all times without worrying if your faith will be accepted. You also have the power to pursue every dream and every desire God has placed in you, nothing is impossible in God's will. The word of God tells us, *"Thou shalt decree a thing and it shall be established."* (Job 22:28.) Praise God for that power he gave!

If you are going through a trying season in your life, I pray that it passes soon, and that you will be victorious on every side. May God saturate you with grace and withhold no good thing from you. May it solidly come to your mind that you are of sound judgment; wisdom and knowledge. In Christ, you have the power to speak that everything in your life bow down to Gods perfect will, and nothing else. That being said, child of God, do not ever take it for granted that all you have, all you can do, is not because of your own might or righteousness, but purely because of God's grace. We are winning because of God's grace, for without God we are nothing. When we are victorious, it is not because 'we believed in ourselves,' but because we believed in God's sovereign power.

I pray that your eyes are open to the sure instruction and comfort that is in God's word as God's word has a way of bringing us back to a place of strength. God's word is the quickest means of accessing strength in time of need. The same way a timely word is intimate, is the same way God shows us the way. Do not be fooled, go to God's word for answers about your life.

"Evil men understand not judgment: but they that seek the Lord understand all things." ~ Proverbs 28:5

See what it is about Christianity and the reality of a God head is that what *we* think is not everything there is to think about. While we are quick to dig into self-help and individualistic can-do mentalities, we are quickly falling into the same trap that Adam and Eve fell into, Lucifer tempted; 'If you eat from this tree you will have the power to be just like God.' In our world today, how many messages are telling us to believe in ourselves and feel no need for God? If you do this, your life will never be the same, if you try my diet, you will never gain weight again, start your own business and never work under authority, if you want to know what God has in store for you, read my book, run for a cure, save the planet. It is quite heartbreaking.

My prayer is that the world begins to realize, that we simply need God.

We have a mighty God to serve, and when we realize what He has done for us, we cannot afford not to bring before him the best. I have so many lost opportunities in life. I got into the tennis school team in my first year of high school, but lost all my matches because I did not fully give myself to the game. I chaired a student Christian group that started dwindling when I was starting my term, a year after I graduated the group dissolved altogether at my school. When I went to college, I was very one-sided about where I wanted my career to go thereafter, and so did not fully apply myself in the moment. When I graduated, all that I had planned the past four years, did not happen the way I thought it would. I was somewhat overly modest in my formative years and never mastered the life skill of being assertive; setting goals and achieving them and I really did not know how to enjoy my life with all the changes it brought. It is the same thing with Christianity, we keep missing out on great moments with God simply because we are not transforming to become men of valour, like Daniel, David, Paul and Peter, the list is endless.

May the Lord give you victory in your life. Sometimes your victory may be merely in the passing of time, and your ability to stand saying God I love you and I will still believe in you. While waiting, we ought to seek after joy, and to reflect joy, because that is a fruit of the spirit. When others see your faith in God during your darkest hour, you bear fruit for the kingdom. While we are praying for a breakthrough, we ought to watch out against obsessing over the desire coming to pass, so much that we miss the teachings God throws along the way. After seeking first the kingdom of God, our hearts desires are surely ours.

May the Lord fight anything that tries to exalt itself

above the Almighty's Word over your life. May God instruct you in the night seasons, which way you should go, to the left or to the right. The enemy is constantly finding ways to keep us in unbelief. When we try to speak things that are not as though they already were, he counter-veils by making things that were not appear as though they were. The devil is a liar, and as for the body of Christ, of which you and I belong, we will believe one report, that of the Lord Jehovah who brought plagues upon a whole nation for the injustice done to those He loved. The same God who brought Israel out of bondage, is the same God who created heaven and earth, of whom we are now adopted and call Abba Father because of the blood of Christ, through whom when we pray we receive what we ask for. Halleluja! We choose to believe that our prayers prevaileth much, we choose to believe that it is not because of who we are, or what man can do, but by the Spirit of the living God that we, like Christ, will also win the battle waged by Lucifer against all mankind. We will not be careful as we proclaim that it shall be well with us who trust God!

To our God, we say, 'Let not your power be spoken less of O mighty God, let not your people stand ashamed, let not your face be turned aside, but come to us, forgive us, and reign over us, be jealous with our souls, with our health, with our joy, in the name of Jesus!'

It is well with the believer's soul, a promise that Christ gave, never will he leave us; never will he forsake us.

Ask God to stir up your spirit, that you would grow in confidence about your faith and deeply feel the need to share the goodness of the love of God. In your own life, when all things God do not seem to be working, and when you want to believe but questions and doubt are coming to your head, when you are simply downcast and it is hard to pray, you feel somewhat mad at God… remember when you told your God;

"One thing have I desired, that will I seek…that I may dwell in the house of the Lord… to behold His beauty and to inquire in his temple." Psalm 27:4

Go and inquire, go back to your God. When you do not know what to do; trust that God is revealing the way (Christ), the truth (Christ) and the life (Christ). For those times when you do not know the way, speak The Way to your life, when you do not know if it is His will, speak The Truth, and when you feel you are down to nothing, and have nothing, speak The Life (John 14 verse 6). God will help you through every stage of life and every situation, but we need to ask, believe and obey. The bible says think not that He cannot send twelve legions of angels to fight for you, that those who are with us will always be greater than those against us. Remember that Christ said we shall do even mightier works than He…and he turned water into wine and five loaves into food for four thousand. He opened the eyes of the blind, welcomed the outcasts, turned around the lives of sinners, raised the dead and commanded demons to flee. Do you believe that God can help you fulfill your purpose for Him? Then according to your faith, may it be done to you, and help your unbelief!

If you are ready, gird up your loins as a mighty man of valour, and be as shrewd as a serpent, like Jacob, who genetically modified sheep to get more, or his mother Rebekah who quickly arranged for the welfare of his tent dweller of a son, like the prostitute Rahab who asked, what's in it for me? Like David who only fought battles for His God, and had the murderer of king Saul killed…like Jesus, who instructed his disciples not to cast pearls before swine…The mystery of God, is utterly confounding isn't it: yet His love endures forever, which side will you choose?

Choose to trust and obey, for there is no other way to be happy in Jesus. I praise the Lord for all He is doing in your life. I know that God will lead you gently into the next reality of your life and I hope it will be an exciting one! As you walk on the journey to serve the kingdom of God, "Make your efforts intense; sustain them and make necessary changes to make them effective."

*

My wish for this generation…

"All nations whom thou hast made shall come and worship before thee, O Lord; and shall glorify thy name. For thou are great, and doest wondrous things: thou art God alone. Teach me thy way, O Lord; I will walk in thy truth: unite my heart to fear thy name." ~ Psalm 86:9-11

"I have set watchmen upon thy walls, o Jerusalem, which shall never hold their peace day nor night: ye that make mention of the Lord, keep not silence." ~ Isaiah 62:6

"How beautiful upon the mountains are the feet of him that bringeth good tidings, that publisheth peace; that bringeth good tidings of good, that publisheth salvation; that saith unto Zion, Thy God reigneth!" ~ Isaiah 52:7

"And what shall I more say? for the time would fail me to tell of Gedeon, and of Barak, and of Samson, and of Jephthae; of David also, and Samuel, and of the prophets: Who through faith subdued kingdoms, wrought righteousness, obtained promises, stopped the mouths of lions. Quenched the violence of fire, escaped the edge of the sword, out of weakness were made strong, waxed valiant in fight, turned to flight the armies of the aliens." ~ Hebrews 11:32-34

Subdue nations, obtain promises and quench fires, for the kingdom of God, the next empire, is at hand.

Shirleen Wronski is an enthralling writer who makes  the topic of spirituality obliging. Her words come with a strong conviction to bear arms for the undying power of God, in spite of the dynamics of Christianity. Shirleen and her husband Kevin are passionate about the lost coming to Christ, and the saved increasing in their capacity to love God and to grow in the Spirit. For more information, visit www.noreproach.ca.